COLOR THE FRACTIONS

Grade 1 Math Book

Children's Fraction Books

Speedy Publishing LLC
40 E. Main St. #1156
Newark, DE 19711
www.speedypublishing.com

fractions are fun!

Let's learn them!
good luck!

A fraction indicates a part of a whole. Fractions have a **numerator** and a **denominator**.

$$\frac{a}{b}$$

a ← numerator

b ← denominator

The **denominator** indicates the number of parts that the whole has been divided into.

The **numerator** indicates the number of parts that you have.

Example:

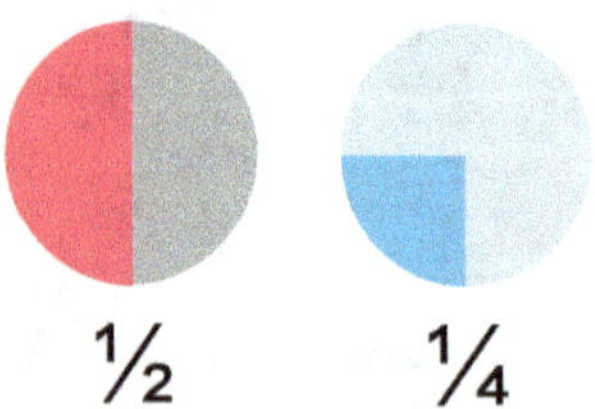

MATCHING FRACTIONS TO A PICTURE

What fraction of each shape is colored?
Circle the correct answer.

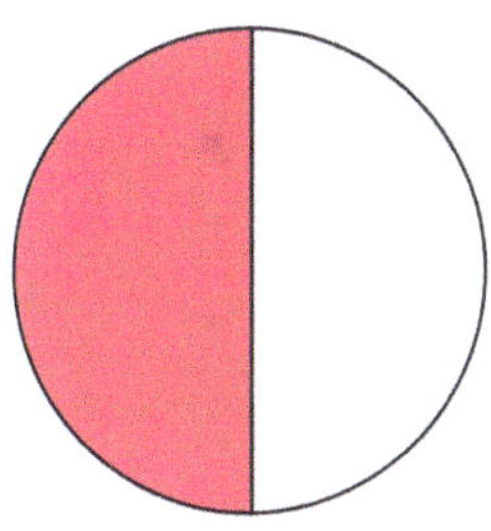

$\frac{1}{4}$ $\frac{1}{2}$ $\frac{2}{4}$ $\frac{2}{3}$

$\frac{1}{4}$ $\frac{1}{3}$ $\frac{3}{3}$ $\frac{2}{3}$

$\frac{1}{4}$ $\frac{2}{3}$ $\frac{2}{4}$ $\frac{4}{4}$

MATCHING FRACTIONS TO A PICTURE

What fraction of each shape is colored?
Circle the correct answer.

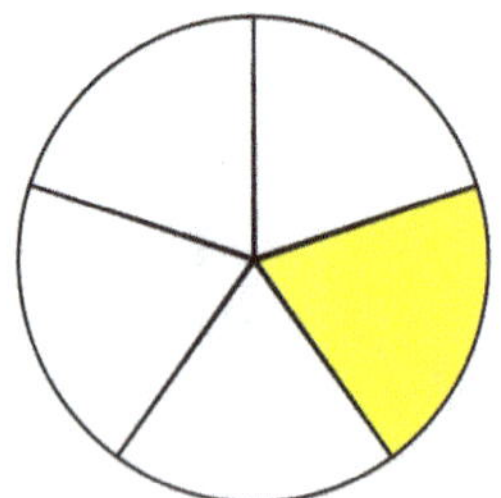

$\frac{1}{5}$ $\frac{1}{7}$ $\frac{4}{6}$ $\frac{2}{4}$

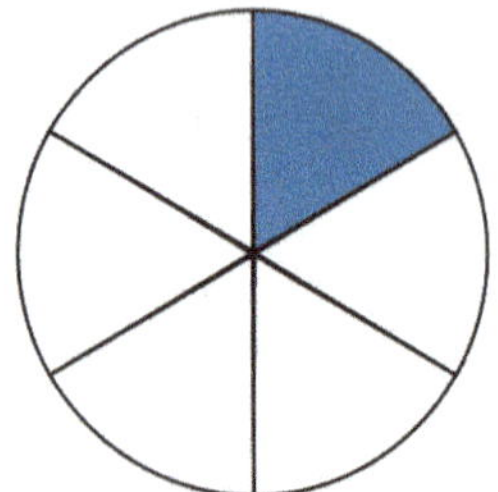

$\frac{1}{4}$ $\frac{1}{3}$ $\frac{3}{5}$ $\frac{1}{6}$

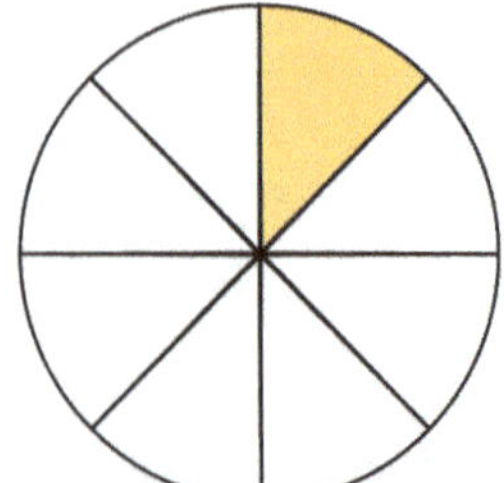

$\frac{1}{4}$ $\frac{2}{3}$ $\frac{1}{8}$ $\frac{4}{4}$

MATCHING FRACTIONS TO A PICTURE

What fraction of each shape is colored?
Circle the correct answer.

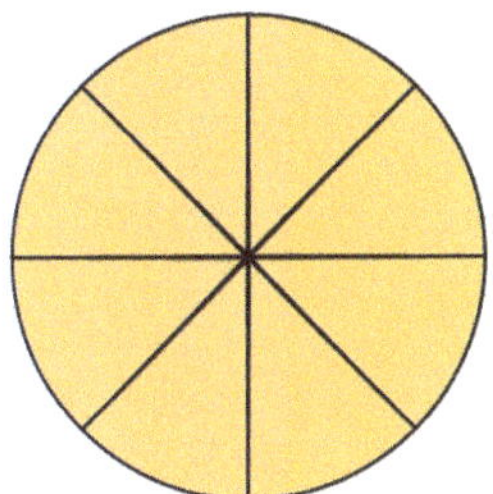

$\frac{1}{4}$ $\frac{5}{5}$ $\frac{8}{8}$ $\frac{3}{4}$

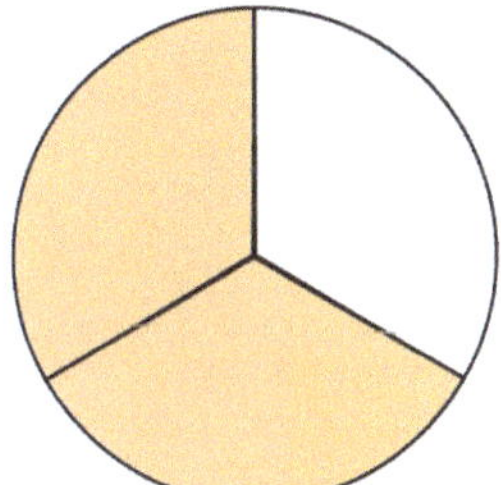

$\frac{4}{4}$ $\frac{1}{3}$ $\frac{3}{3}$ $\frac{2}{3}$

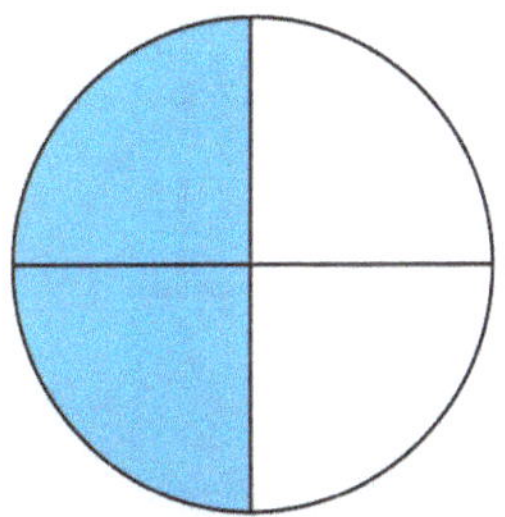

$\frac{1}{4}$ $\frac{2}{3}$ $\frac{2}{4}$ $\frac{6}{6}$

MATCHING FRACTIONS TO A PICTURE

What fraction of each shape is colored?
Circle the correct answer.

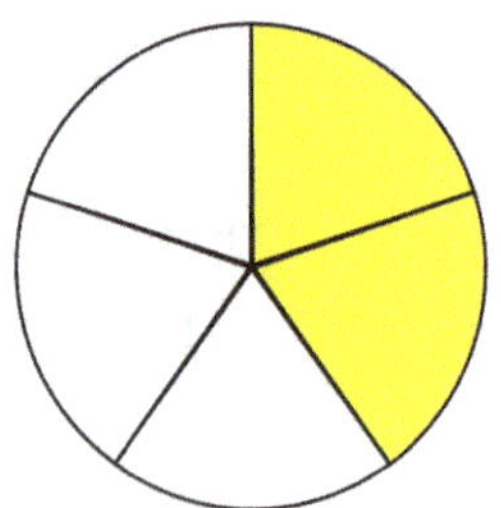

$\frac{5}{7}$ $\frac{1}{2}$ $\frac{2}{5}$ $\frac{2}{3}$

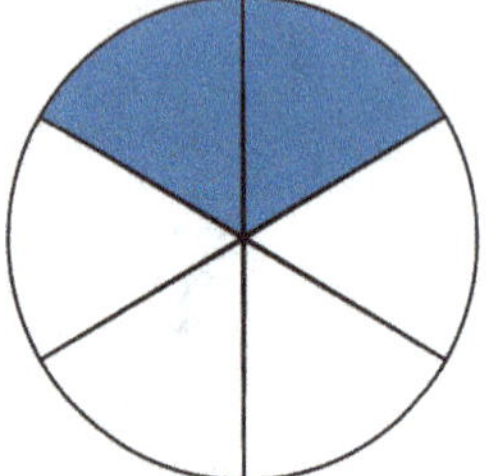

$\frac{1}{4}$ $\frac{2}{6}$ $\frac{3}{3}$ $\frac{5}{7}$

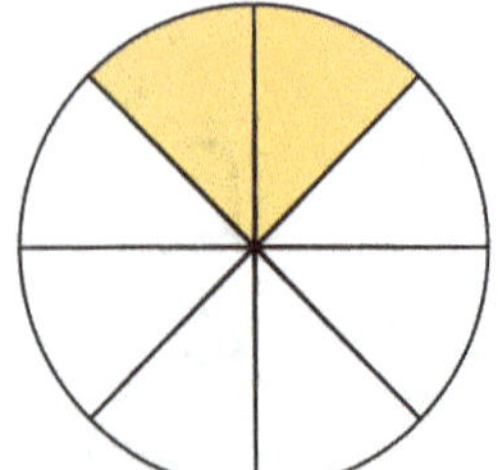

$\frac{2}{8}$ $\frac{2}{3}$ $\frac{2}{4}$ $\frac{4}{7}$

MATCHING FRACTIONS TO A PICTURE

What fraction of each shape is colored?
Circle the correct answer.

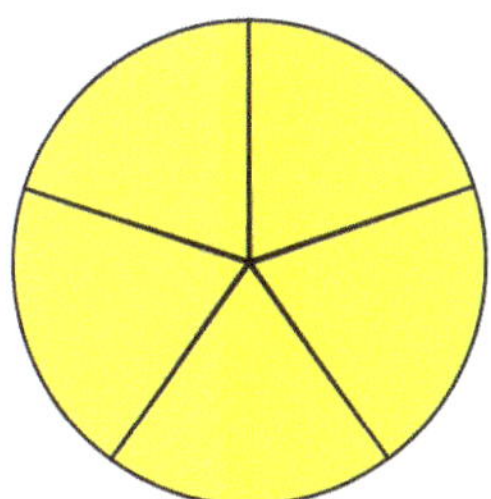

$\frac{5}{5}$ $\frac{1}{2}$ $\frac{2}{4}$ $\frac{2}{3}$

$\frac{1}{4}$ $\frac{1}{3}$ $\frac{3}{3}$ $\frac{4}{5}$

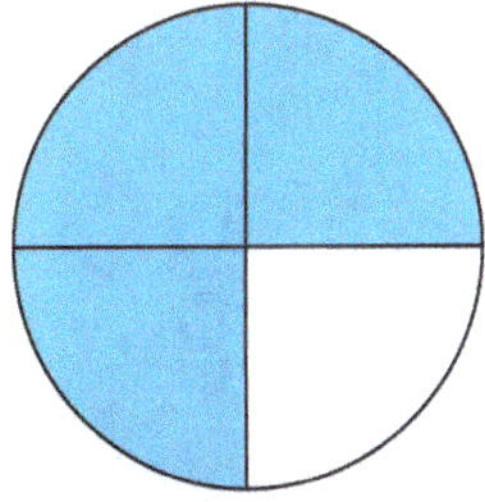

$\frac{1}{4}$ $\frac{2}{3}$ $\frac{2}{4}$ $\frac{3}{4}$

MATCHING FRACTIONS TO A PICTURE

What fraction of each shape is colored?
Circle the correct answer.

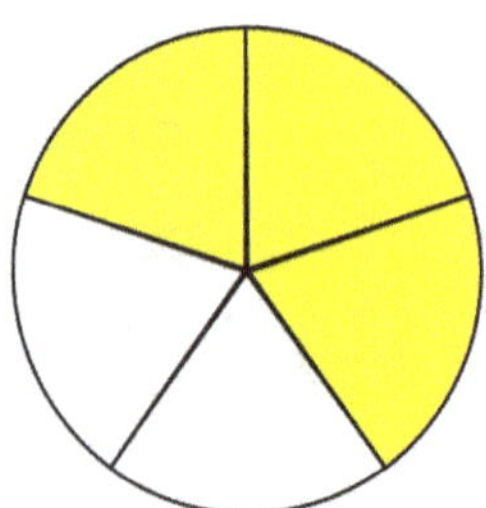

$\frac{4}{7}$ $\frac{1}{2}$ $\frac{3}{5}$ $\frac{2}{3}$

$\frac{1}{4}$ $\frac{1}{3}$ $\frac{3}{6}$ $\frac{3}{7}$

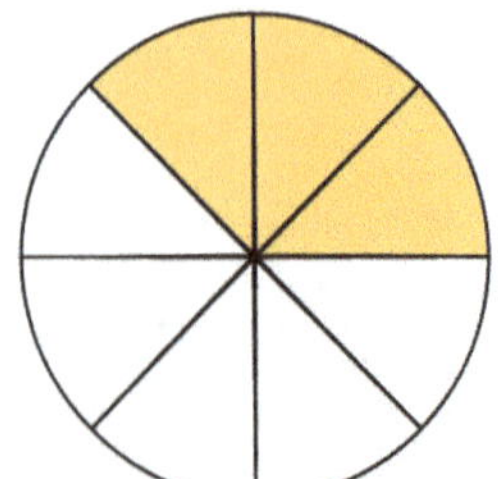

$\frac{1}{4}$ $\frac{3}{8}$ $\frac{2}{4}$ $\frac{6}{8}$

MATCHING FRACTIONS TO A PICTURE

What fraction of each shape is colored?
Circle the correct answer.

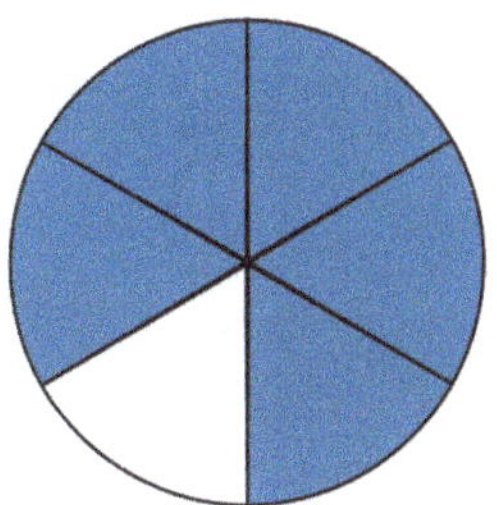

$\frac{6}{7}$ $\frac{1}{2}$ $\frac{5}{6}$ $\frac{2}{3}$

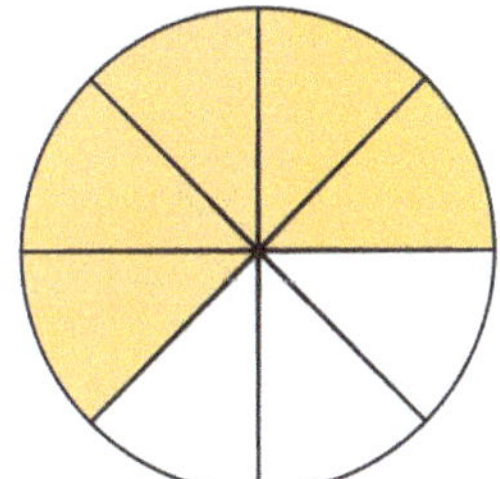

$\frac{5}{8}$ $\frac{1}{3}$ $\frac{3}{3}$ $\frac{5}{7}$

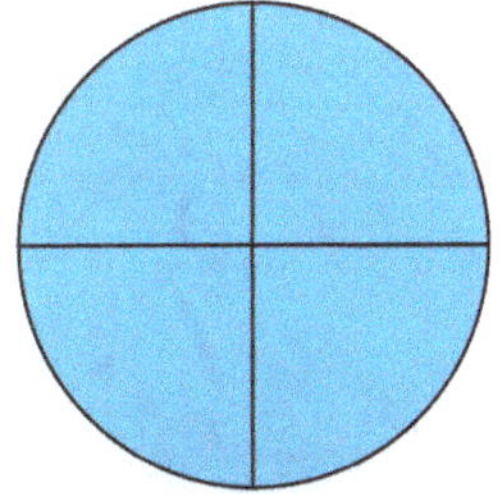

$\frac{1}{4}$ $\frac{2}{3}$ $\frac{2}{4}$ $\frac{4}{4}$

MATCHING FRACTIONS TO A PICTURE

What fraction of each shape is colored?
Circle the correct answer.

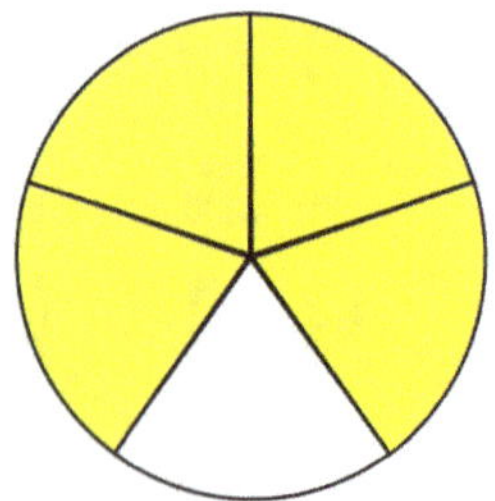

$\frac{4}{5}$ $\frac{1}{2}$ $\frac{1}{6}$ $\frac{5}{6}$

$\frac{1}{4}$ $\frac{4}{6}$ $\frac{3}{3}$ $\frac{6}{6}$

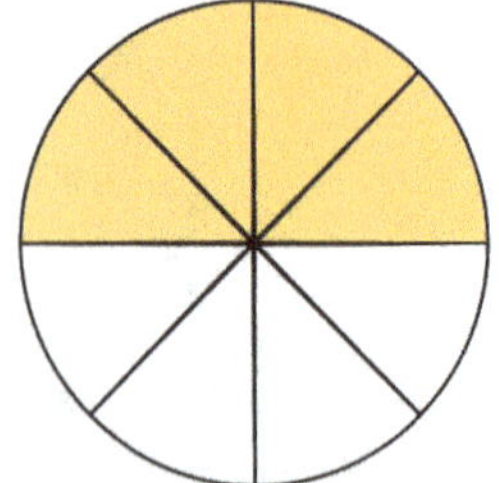

$\frac{4}{8}$ $\frac{2}{3}$ $\frac{2}{4}$ $\frac{6}{7}$

MATCHING FRACTIONS TO A PICTURE

What fraction of each shape is colored?
Circle the correct answer.

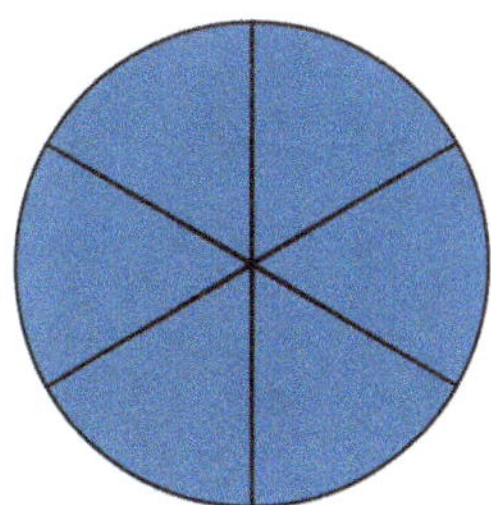

$\frac{6}{6}$ $\frac{1}{2}$ $\frac{2}{4}$ $\frac{1}{6}$

$\frac{8}{9}$ $\frac{1}{3}$ $\frac{3}{3}$ $\frac{6}{8}$

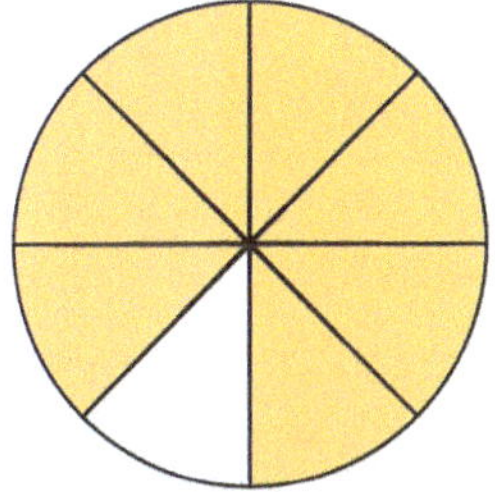

$\frac{1}{4}$ $\frac{5}{6}$ $\frac{2}{4}$ $\frac{7}{8}$

MATCHING FRACTIONS TO A PICTURE

What fraction of each shape is colored?
Circle the correct answer.

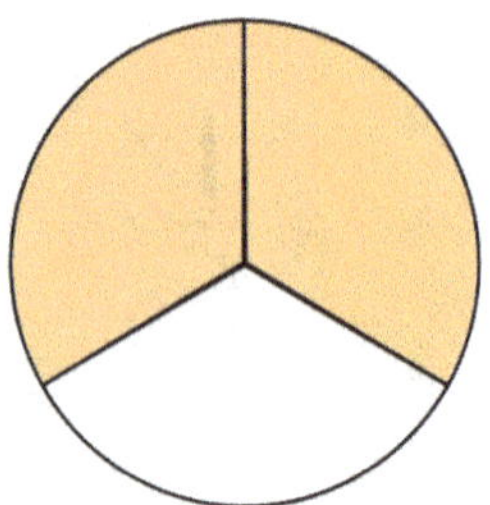

$\frac{5}{5}$ $\frac{1}{2}$ $\frac{2}{4}$ $\frac{2}{3}$

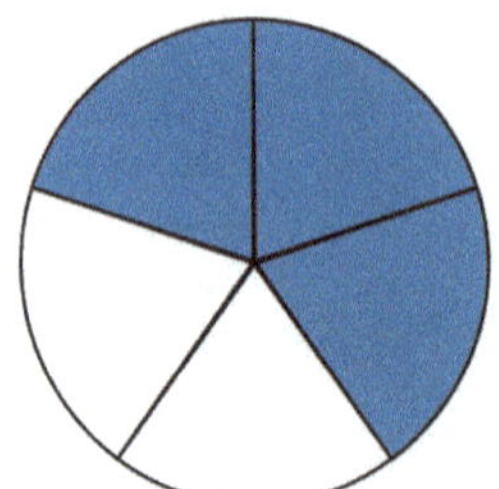

$\frac{3}{5}$ $\frac{1}{3}$ $\frac{3}{3}$ $\frac{5}{6}$

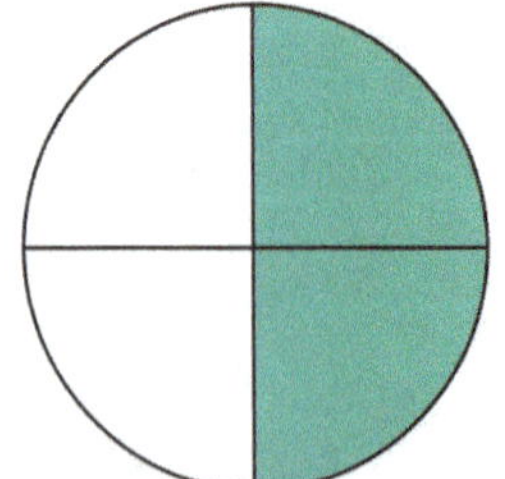

$\frac{4}{7}$ $\frac{2}{3}$ $\frac{2}{4}$ $\frac{3}{4}$

COLORING SHAPES TO SHOW FRACTIONS

Color in the fraction shown of each picture.

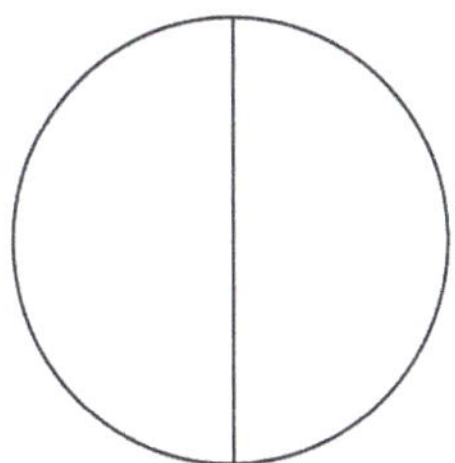

$\frac{1}{2}$

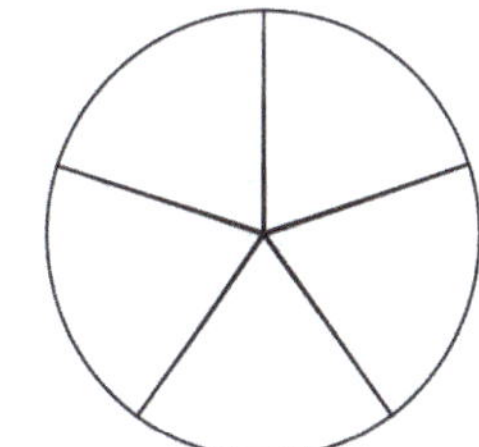

$\frac{1}{5}$

$\frac{1}{3}$

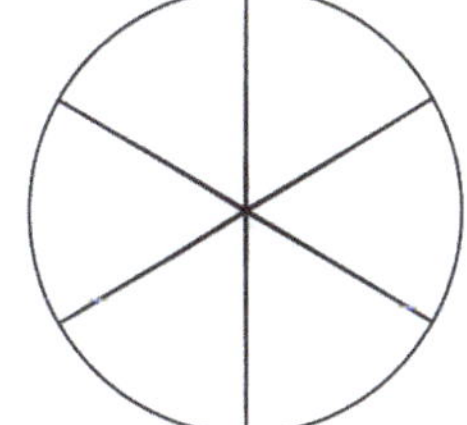

$\frac{1}{6}$

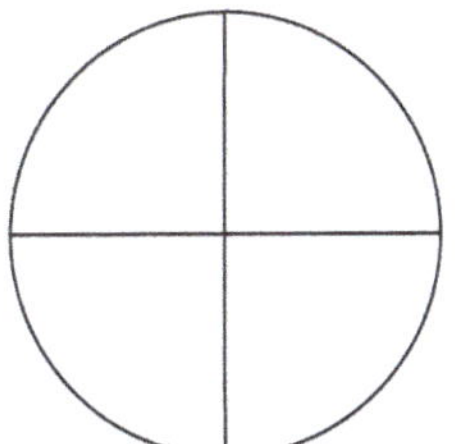

$\frac{1}{4}$

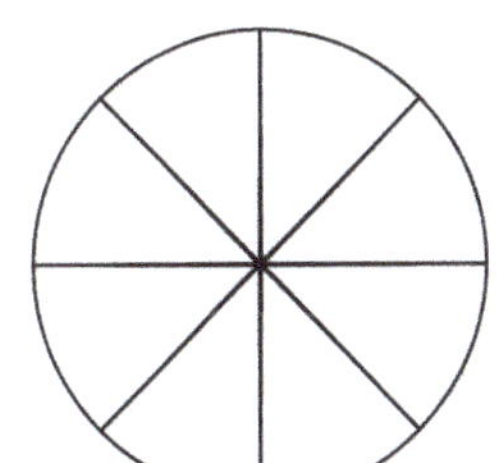

$\frac{1}{8}$

COLORING SHAPES TO SHOW FRACTIONS

Color in the fraction shown of each picture.

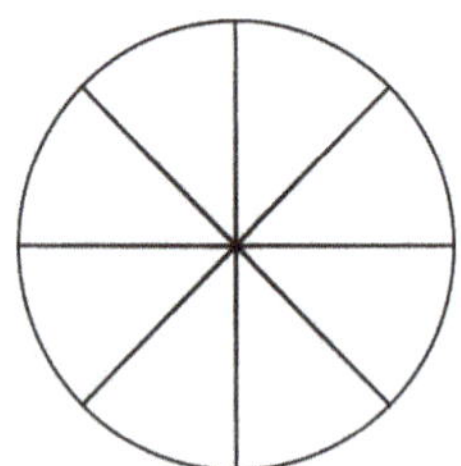

$\frac{2}{8}$

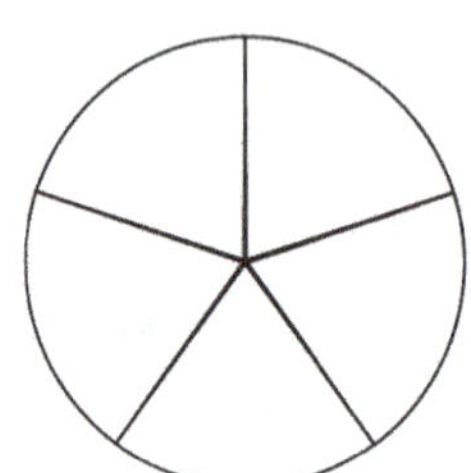

$\frac{2}{5}$

$\frac{2}{3}$

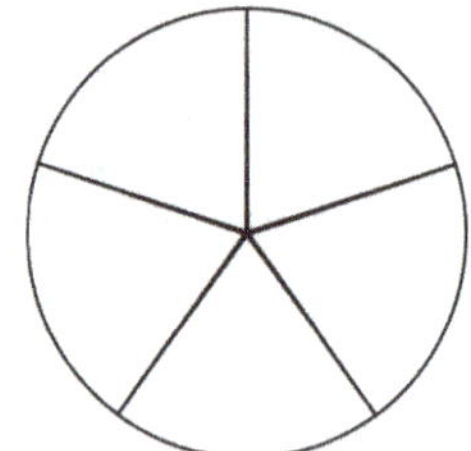

$\frac{2}{5}$

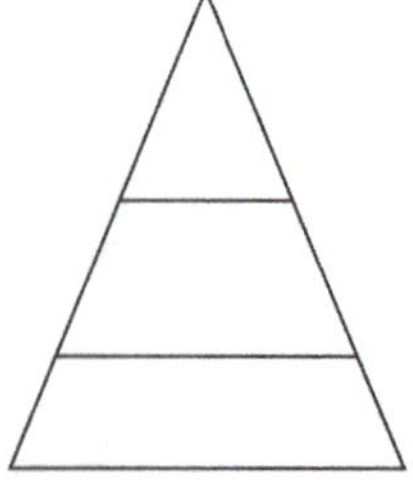

$\frac{2}{3}$

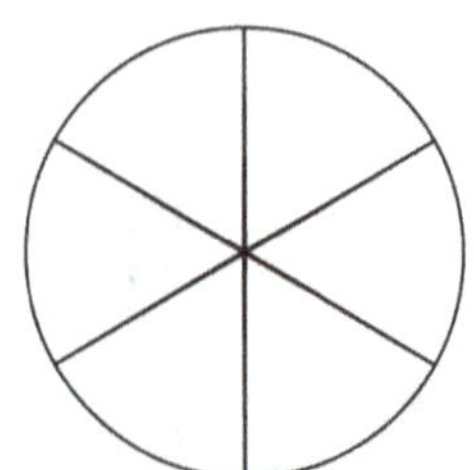

$\frac{3}{6}$

COLORING SHAPES TO SHOW FRACTIONS

Color in the fraction shown of each picture.

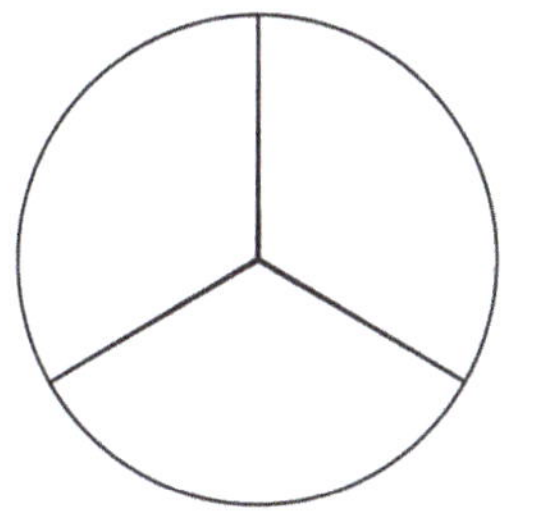

$\frac{3}{3}$

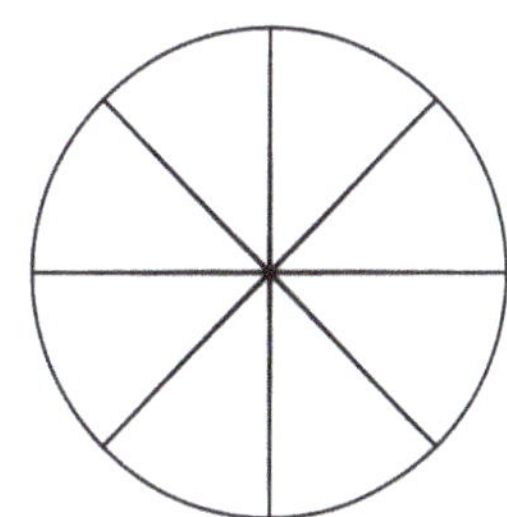

$\frac{4}{8}$

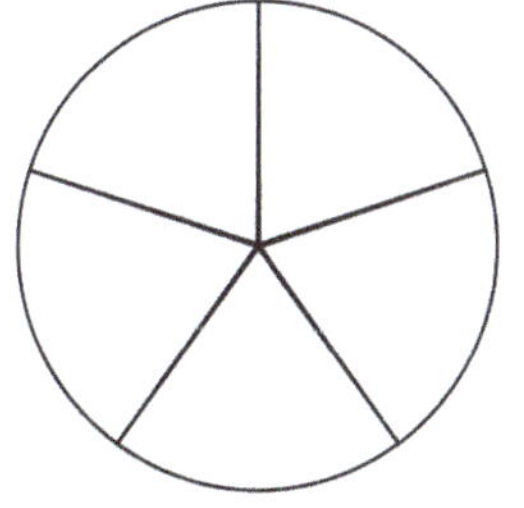

$\frac{5}{6}$

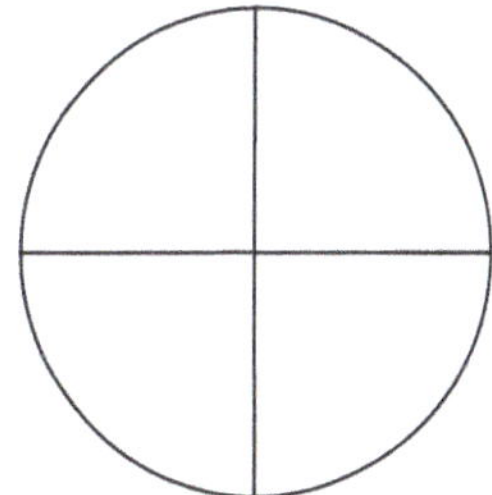

$\frac{2}{4}$

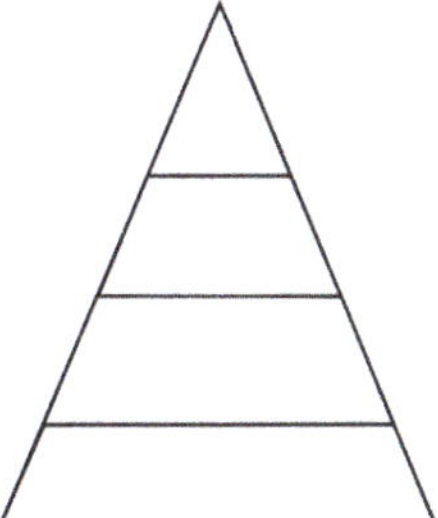

$\frac{1}{4}$

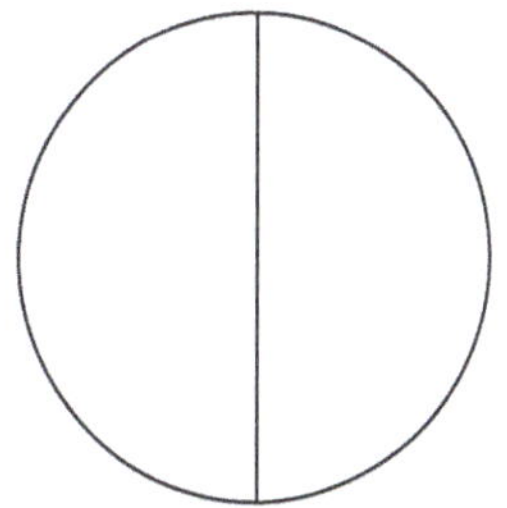

$\frac{1}{2}$

Color in the fraction shown of each picture.

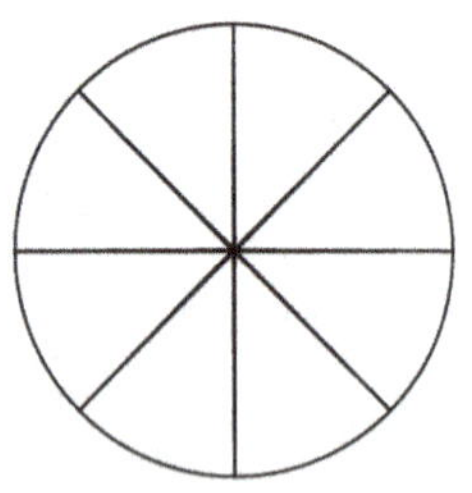

$\frac{5}{8}$

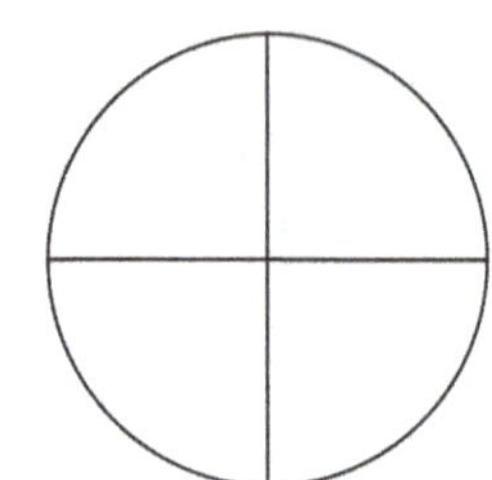

$\frac{3}{4}$

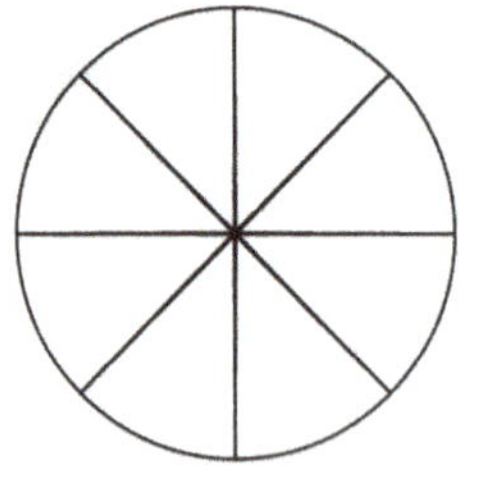

$\frac{6}{8}$

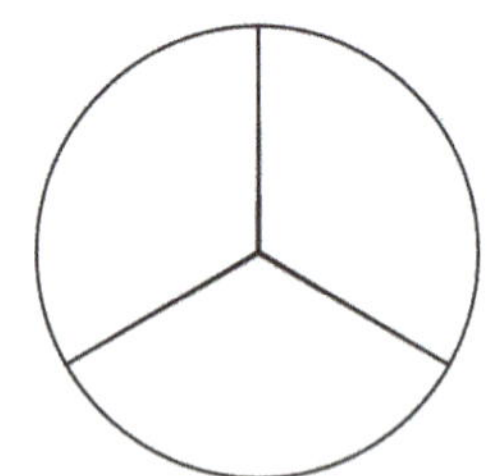

$\frac{2}{3}$

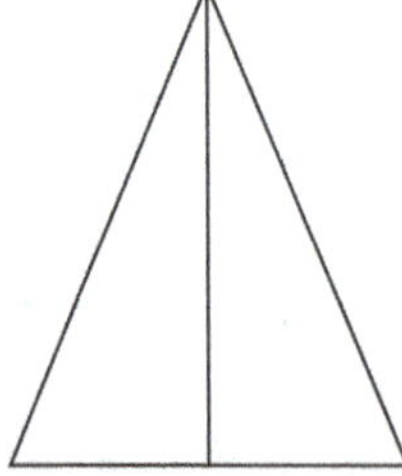

$\frac{2}{2}$

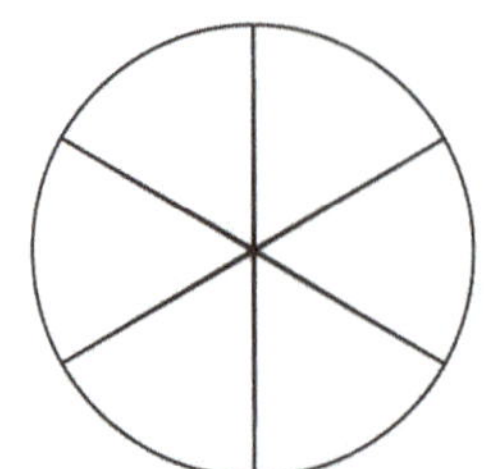

$\frac{5}{6}$

COLORING SHAPES TO SHOW FRACTIONS

Color in the fraction shown of each picture.

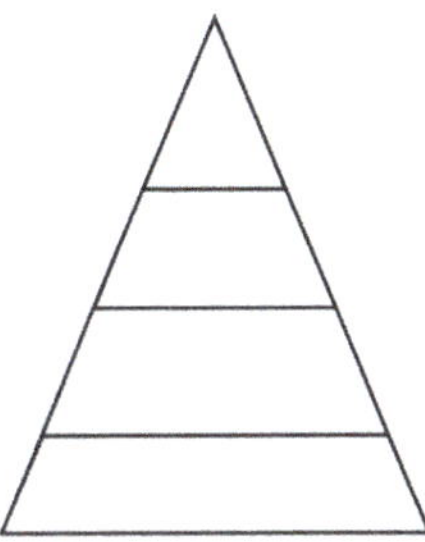

$\frac{1}{4}$

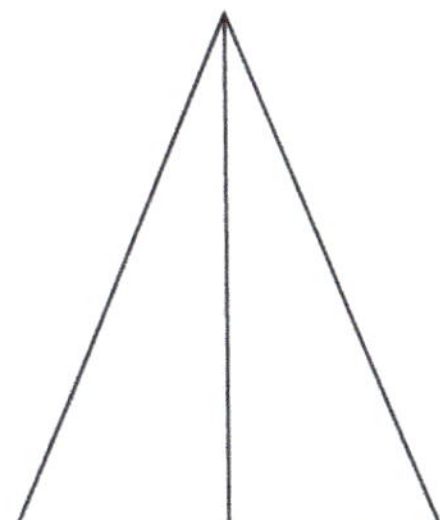

$\frac{1}{2}$

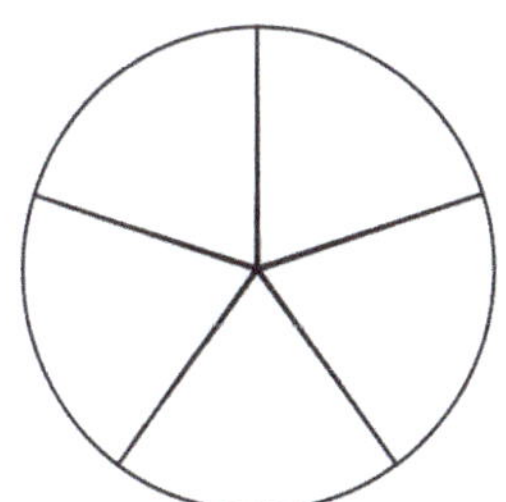

$\frac{3}{5}$

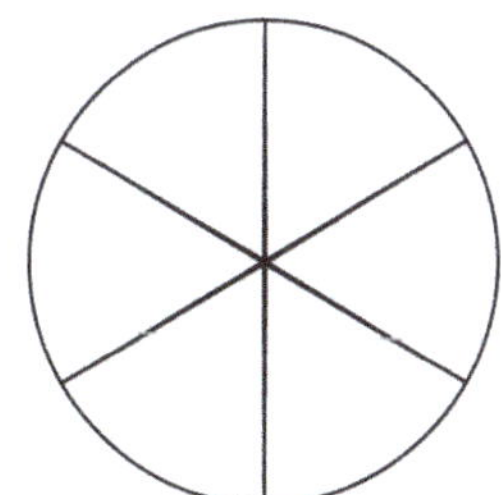

$\frac{4}{6}$

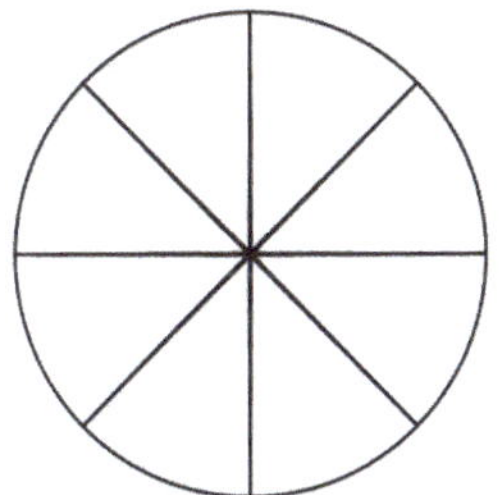

$\frac{3}{8}$

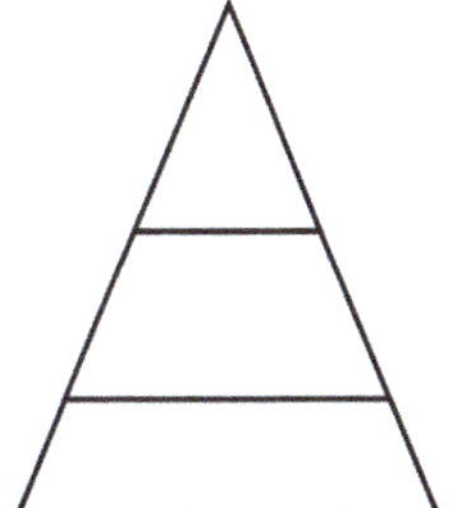

$\frac{1}{3}$

COLORING SHAPES TO SHOW FRACTIONS

Color in the fraction shown of each picture.

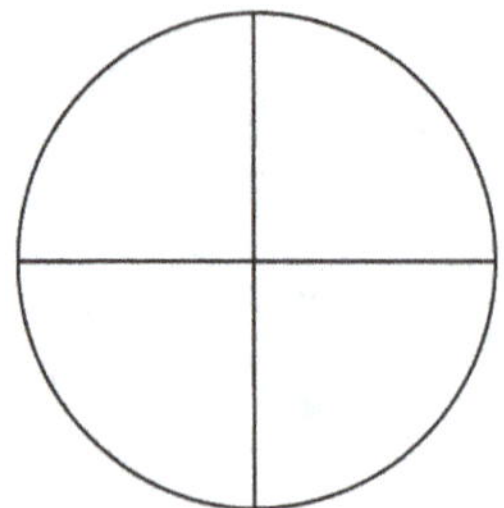

$\frac{4}{4}$

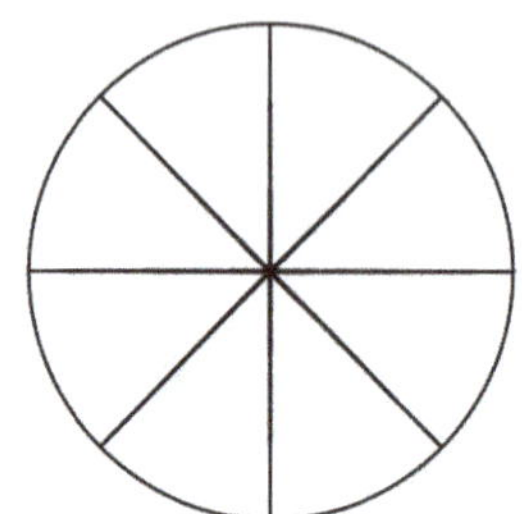

$\frac{7}{8}$

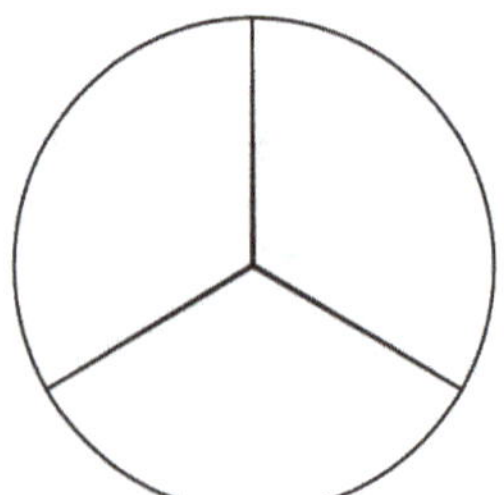

$\frac{3}{3}$

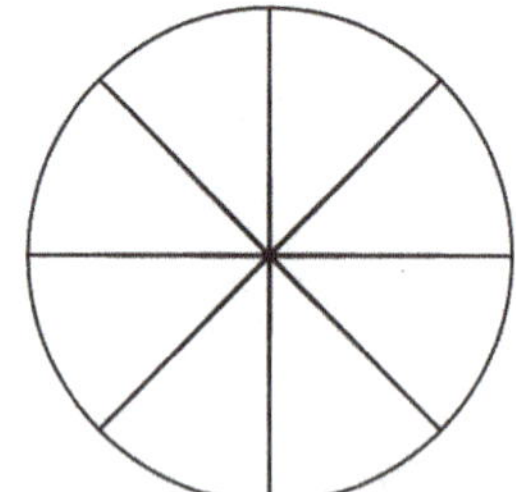

$\frac{8}{8}$

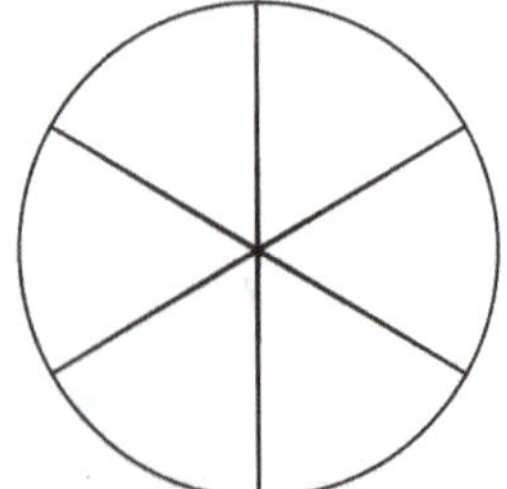

$\frac{6}{6}$

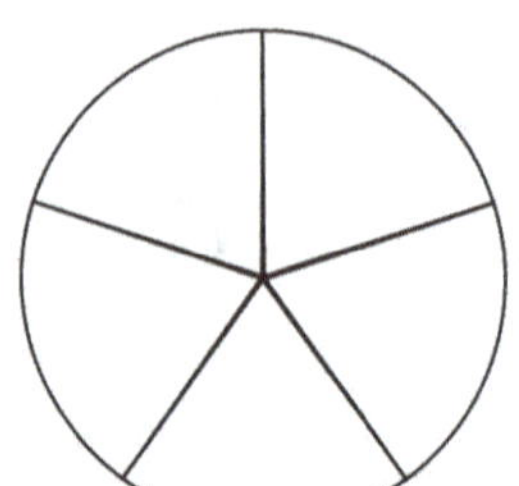

$\frac{5}{5}$

COLORING SHAPES TO SHOW FRACTIONS

Color in the fraction shown of each picture.

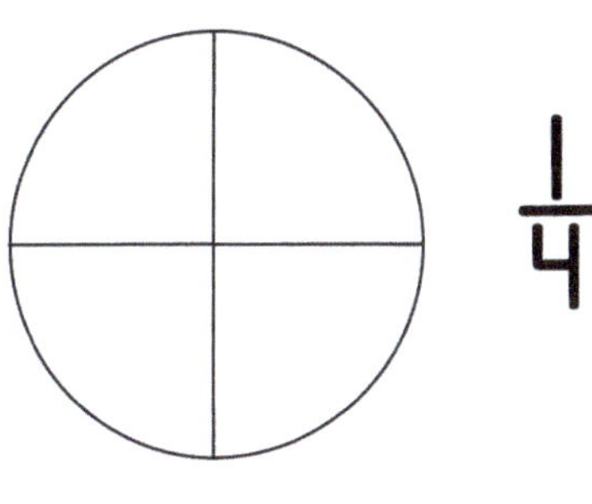

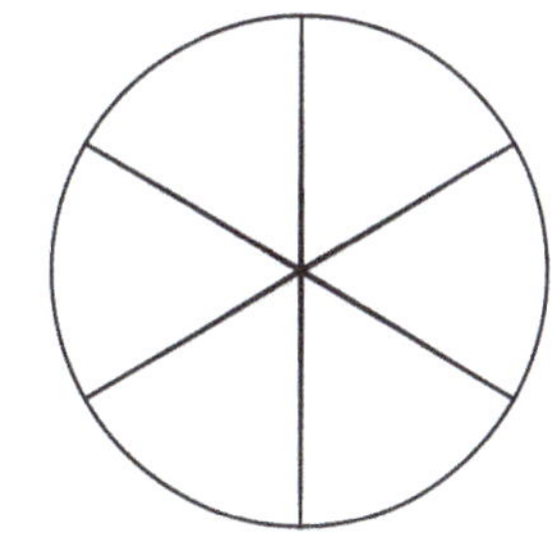

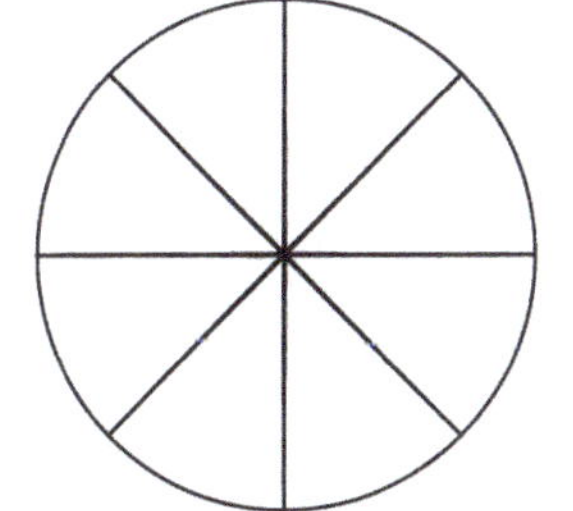

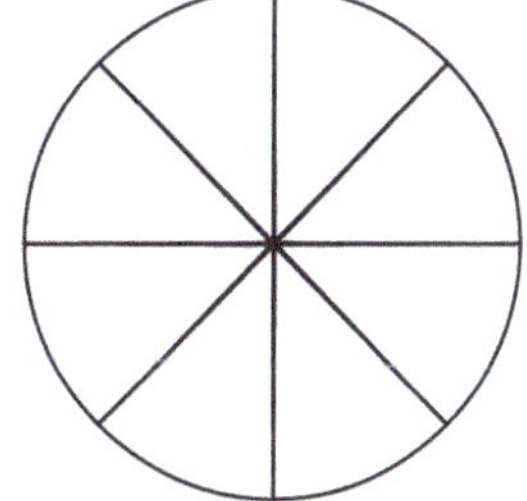

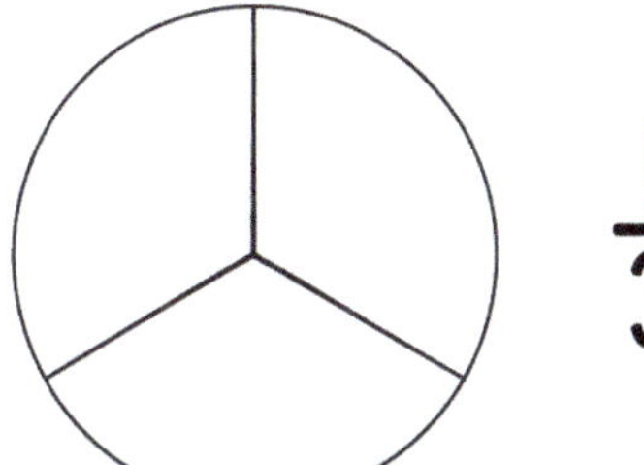

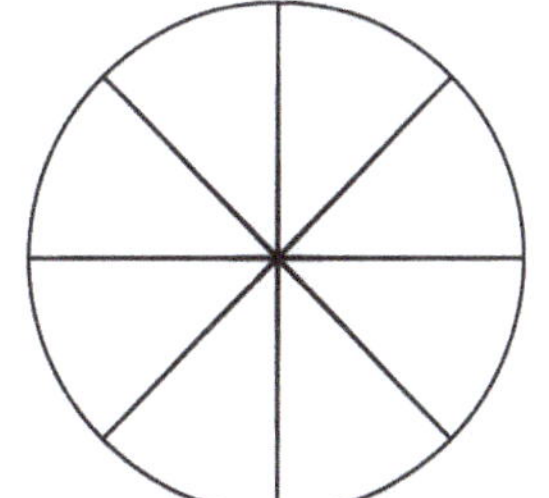

COLORING SHAPES TO SHOW FRACTIONS

Color in the fraction shown of each picture.

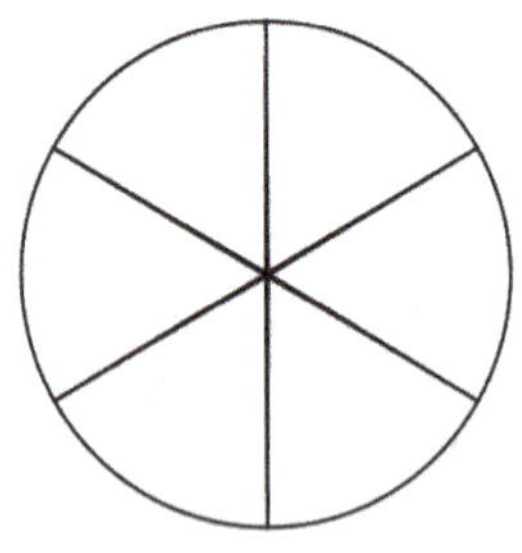

$\frac{1}{6}$

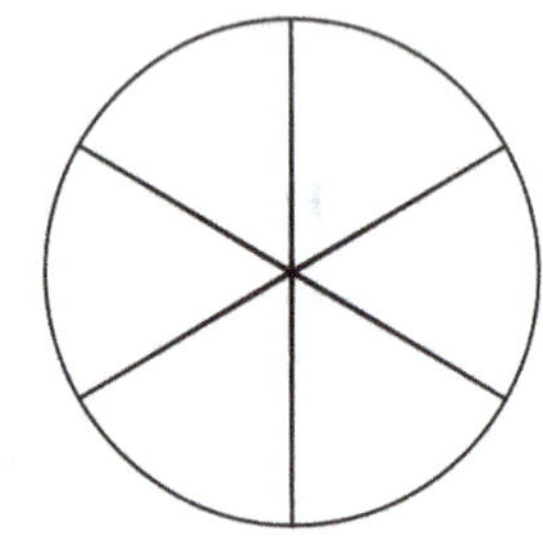

$\frac{2}{6}$

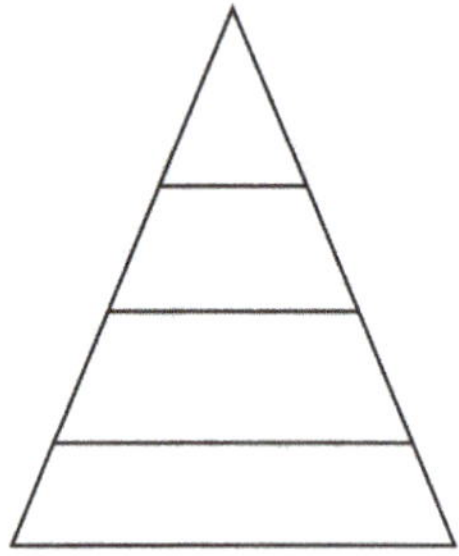

$\frac{4}{4}$

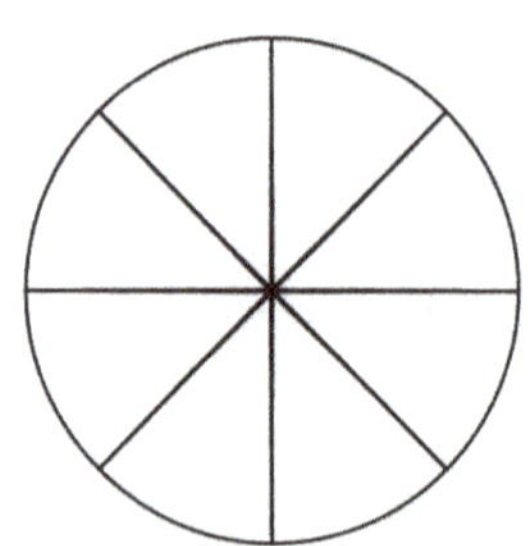

$\frac{1}{8}$

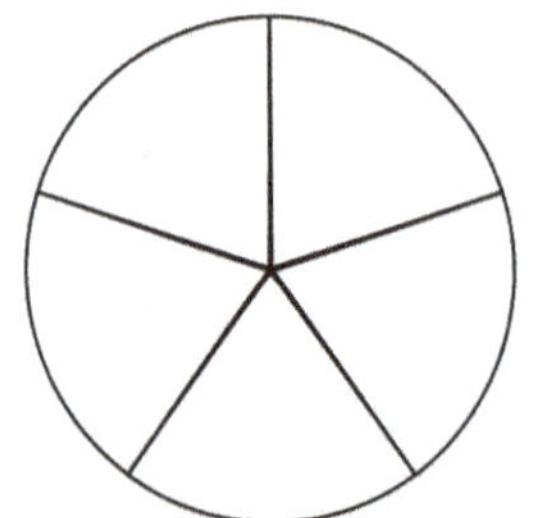

$\frac{3}{5}$

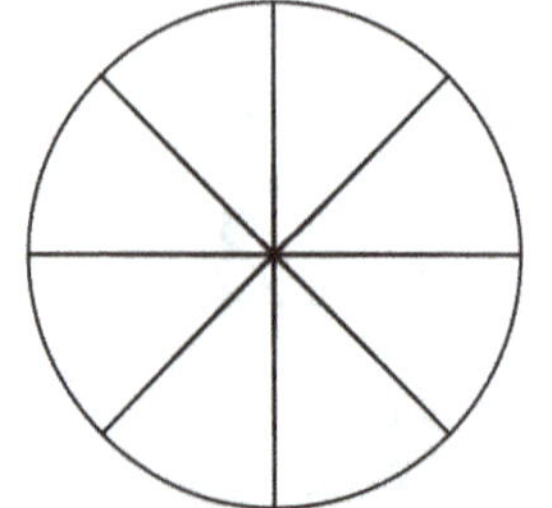

$\frac{4}{8}$

COLORING SHAPES TO SHOW FRACTIONS

Color in the fraction shown of each picture.

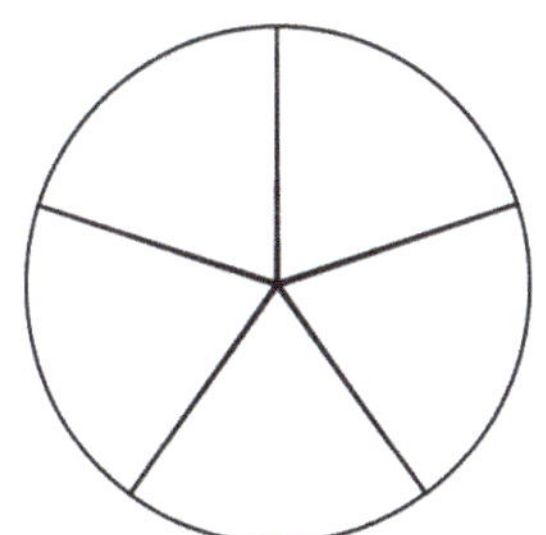

$\frac{3}{5}$

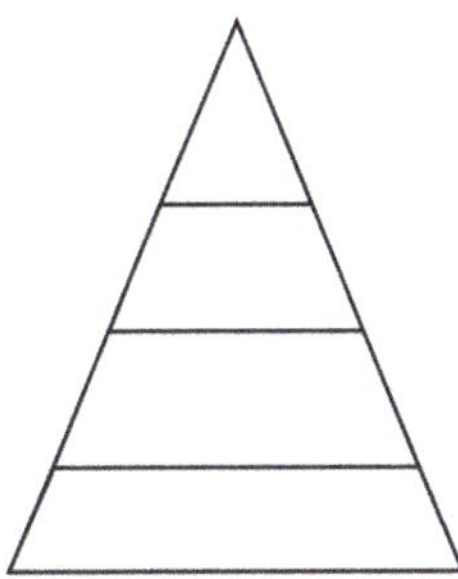

$\frac{3}{4}$

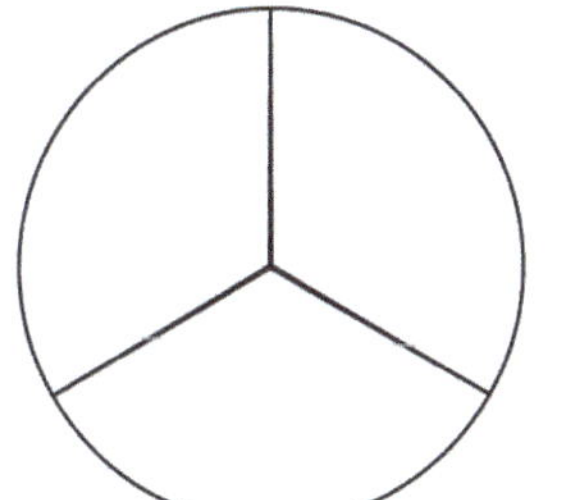

$\frac{2}{3}$

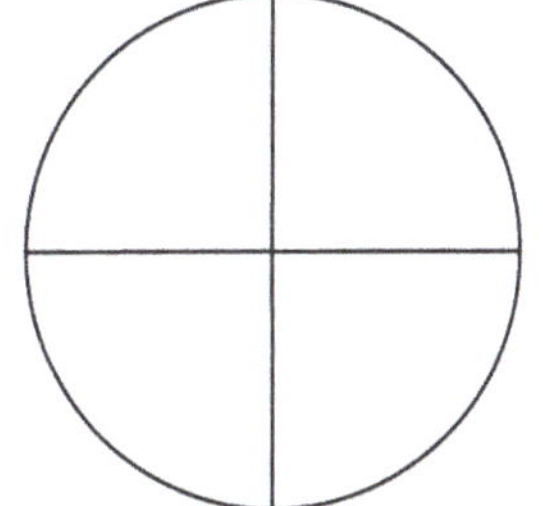

$\frac{2}{4}$

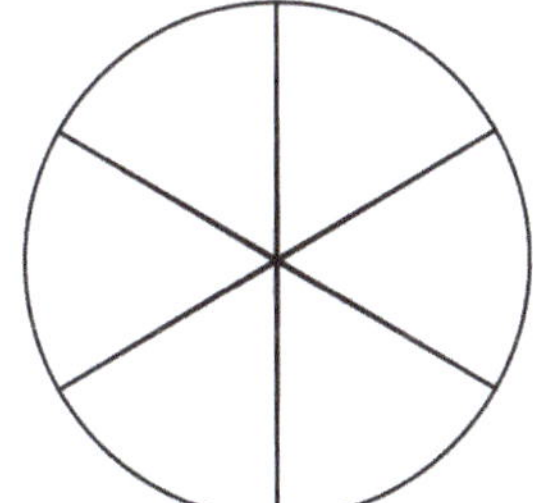

$\frac{2}{6}$

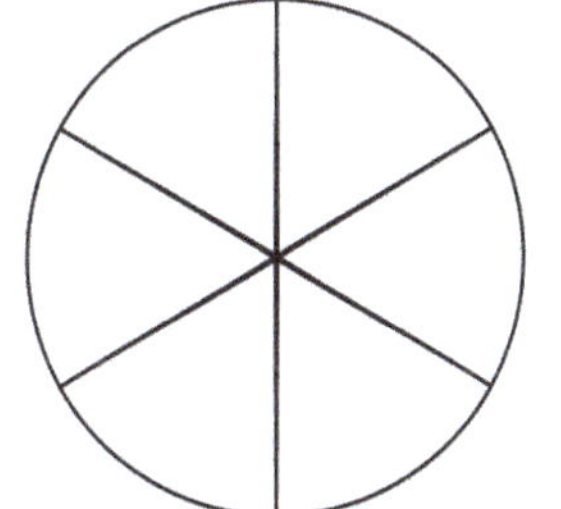

$\frac{3}{6}$

COLORING SHAPES TO SHOW FRACTIONS

Color in the fraction shown of each picture.

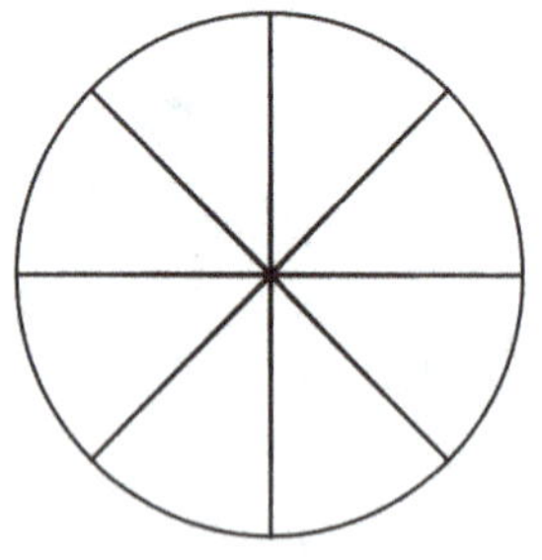

$\frac{4}{8}$

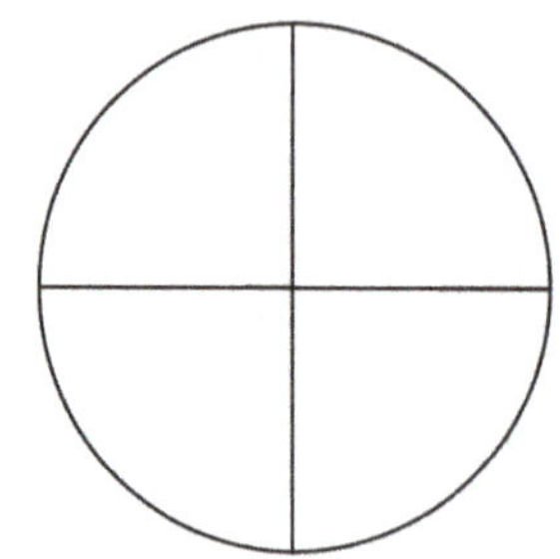

$\frac{2}{4}$

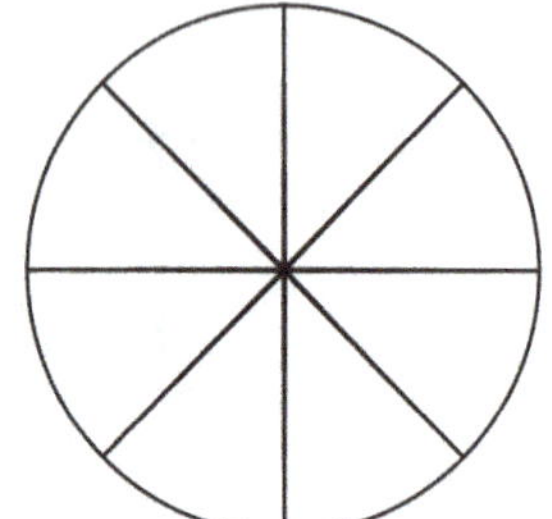

$\frac{3}{8}$

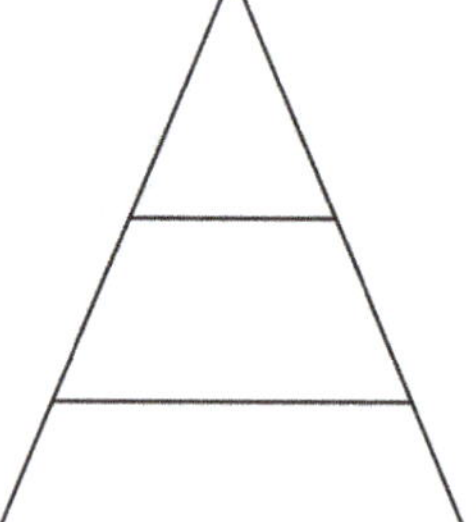

$\frac{2}{3}$

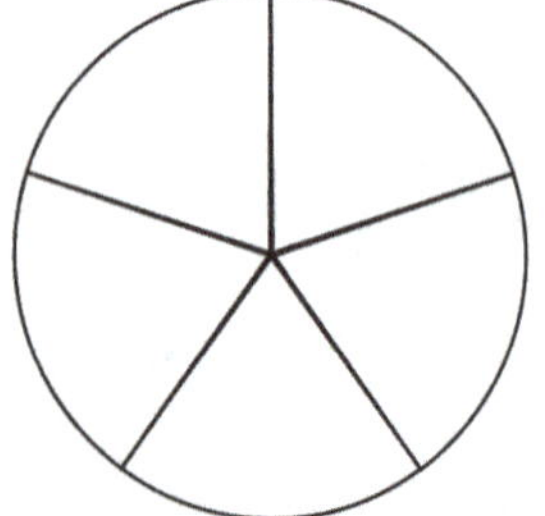

$\frac{2}{5}$

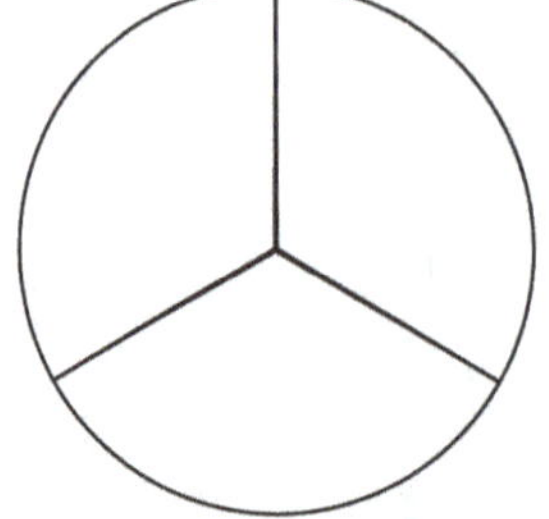

$\frac{1}{3}$

WRITING FRACTIONS

Write the fraction of the shape that is filled in.

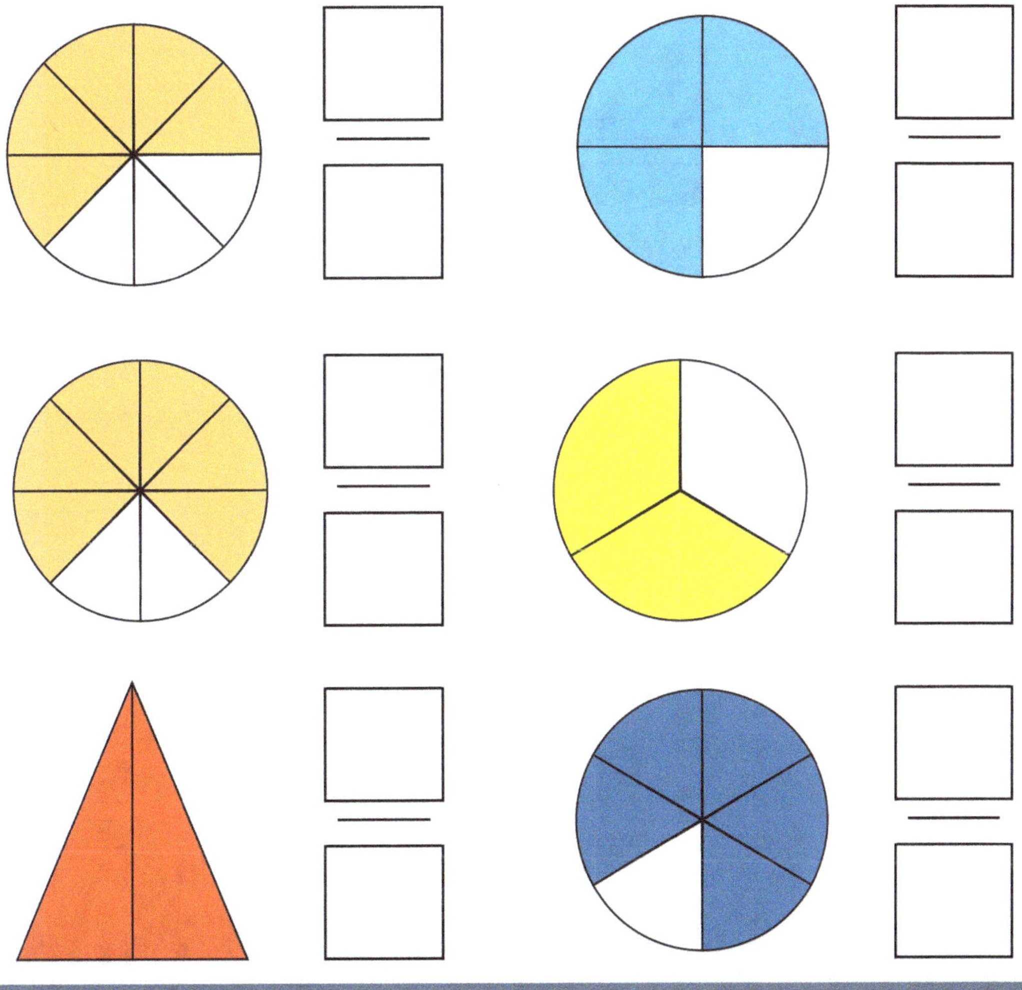

WRITING FRACTIONS

Write the fraction of the shape that is filled in.

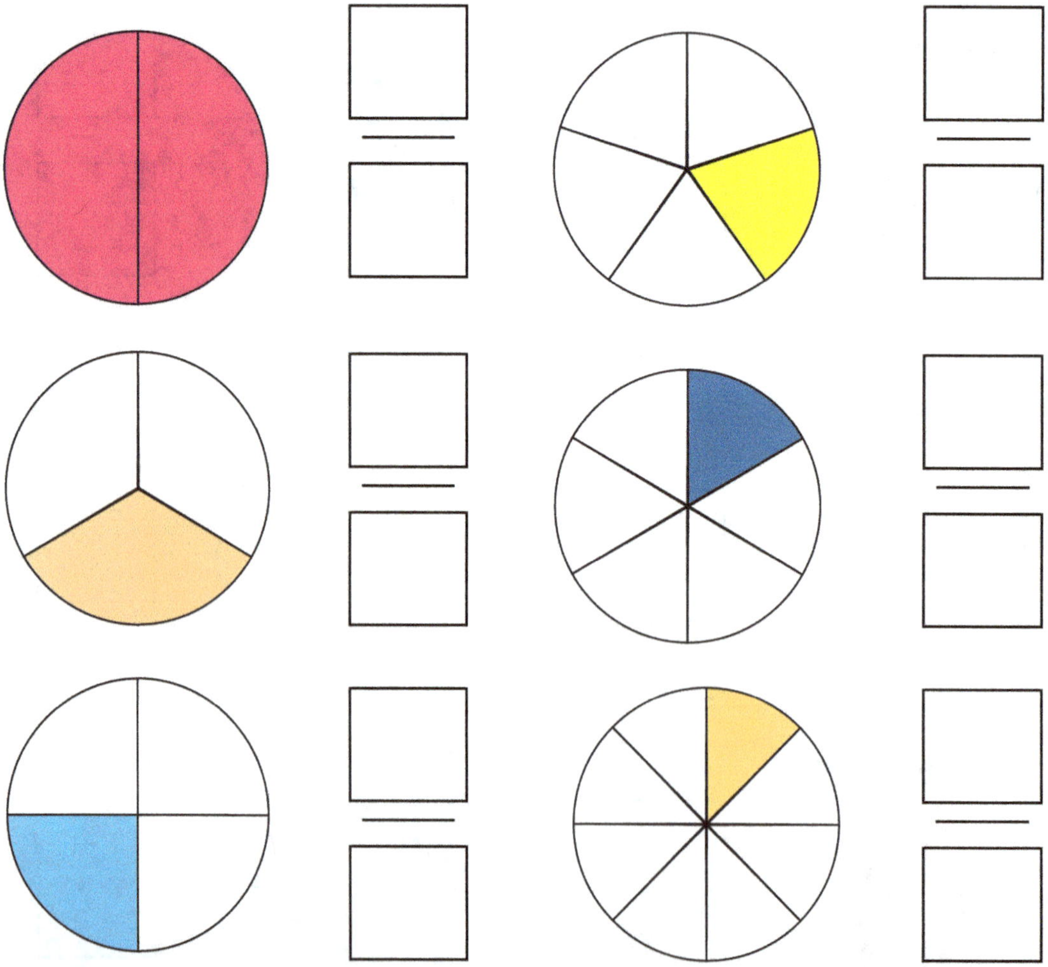

WRITING FRACTIONS

Write the fraction of the shape that is filled in.

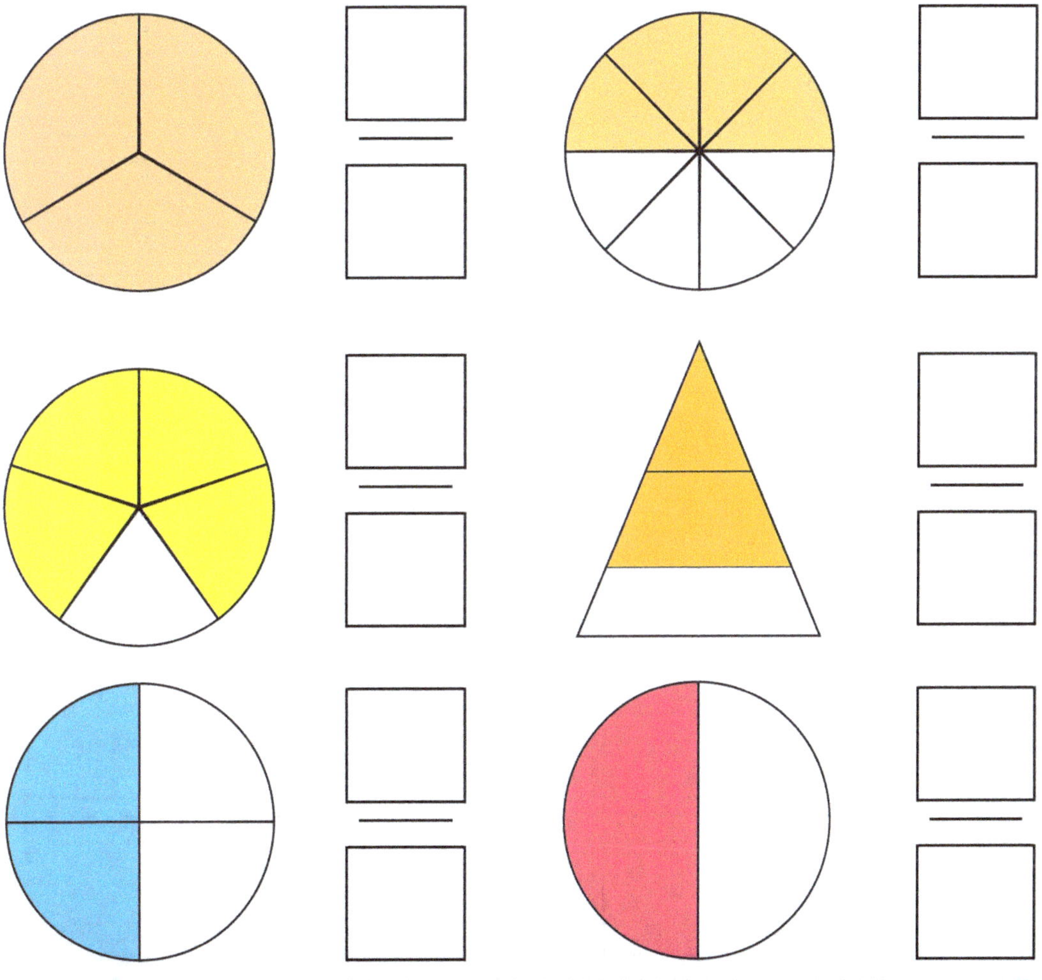

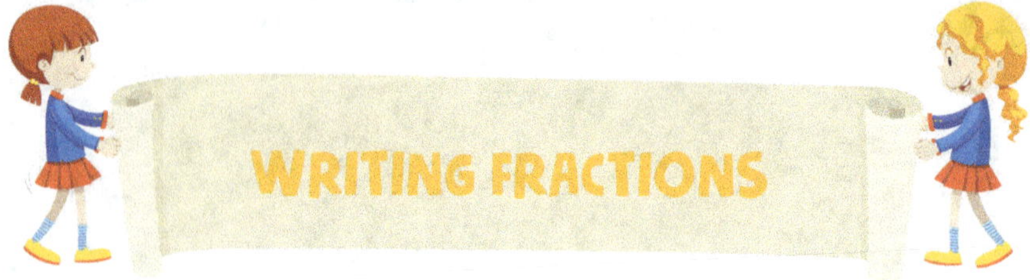

WRITING FRACTIONS

Write the fraction of the shape that is filled in.

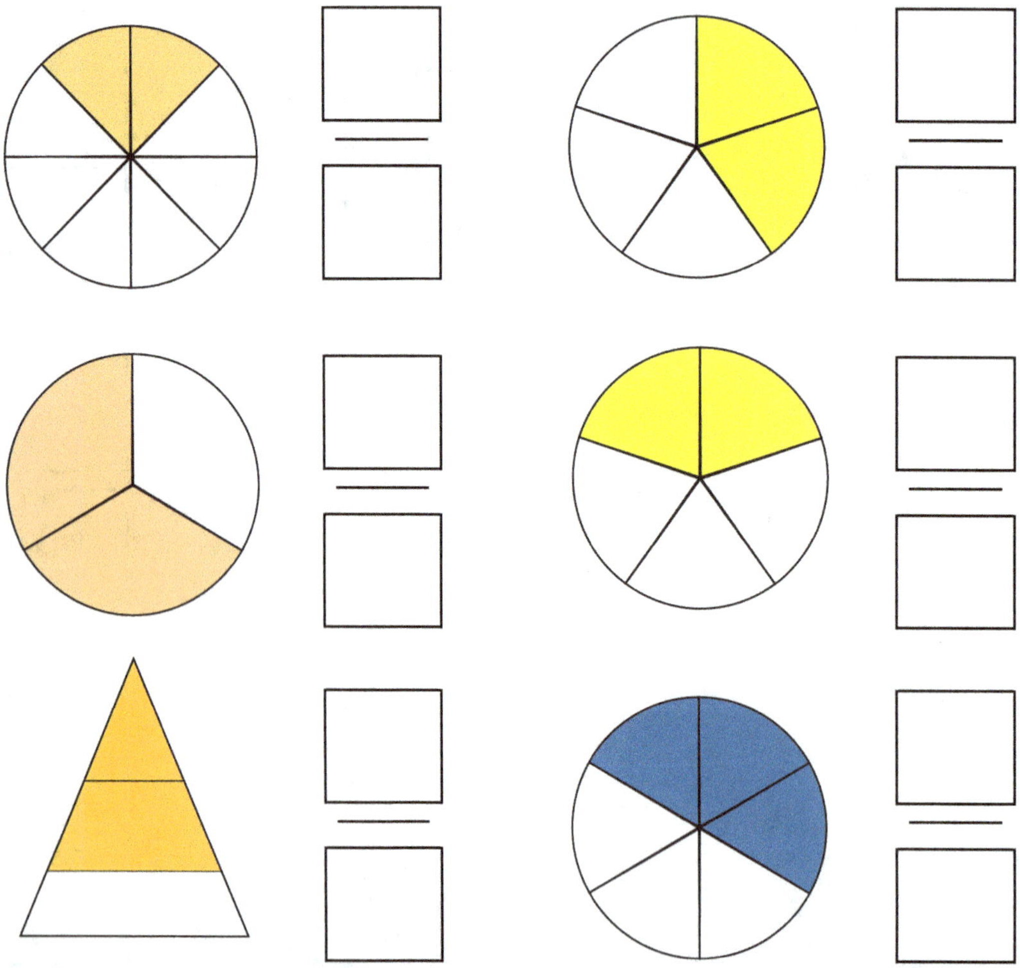

WRITING FRACTIONS

Write the fraction of the shape that is filled in.

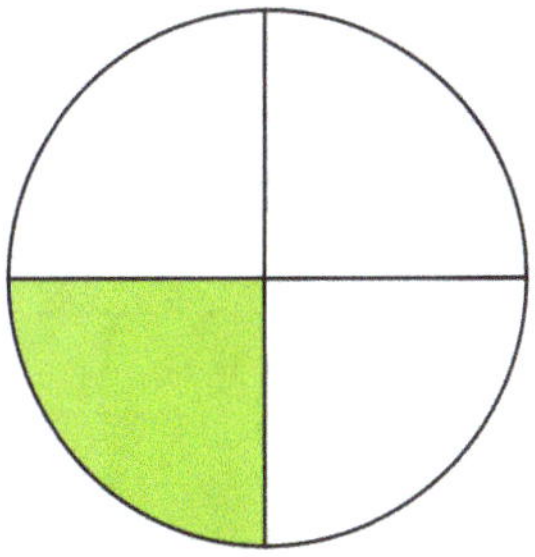

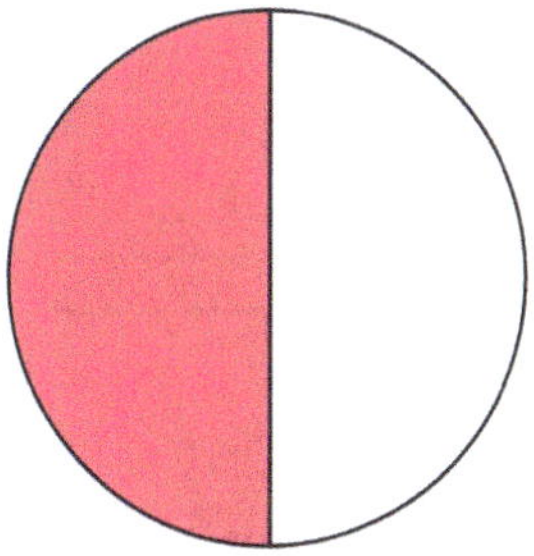

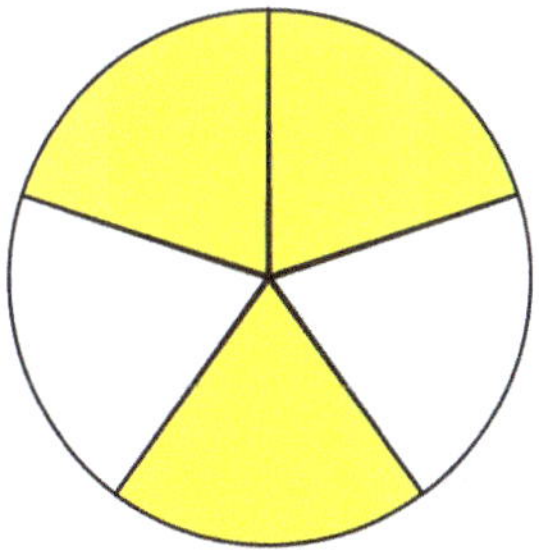

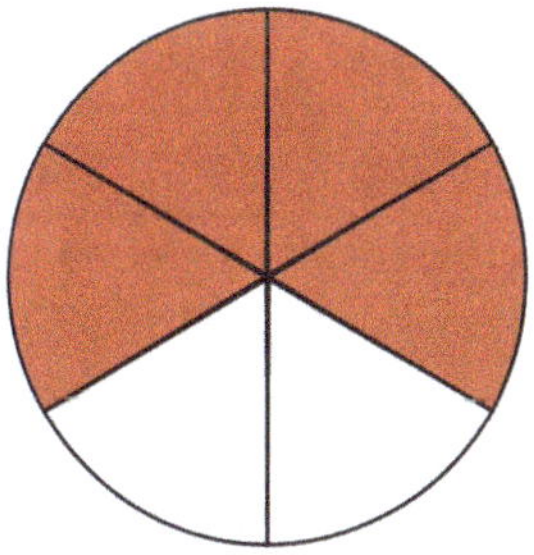

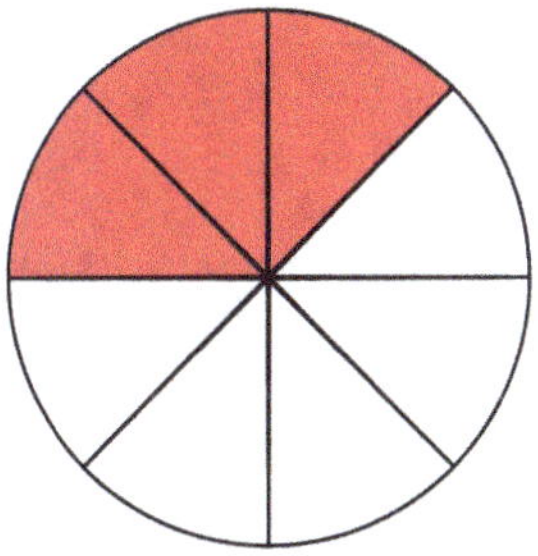

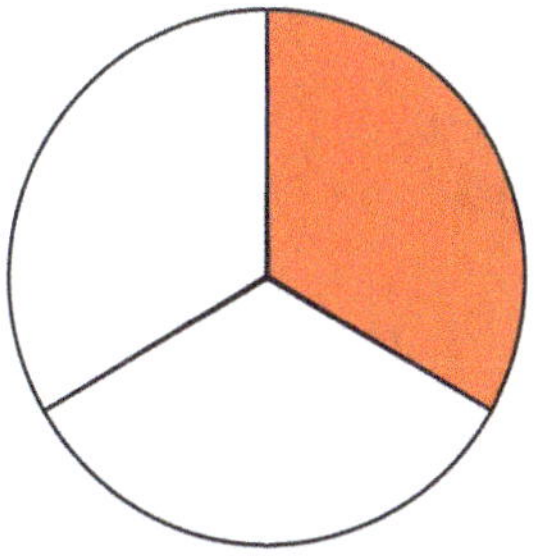

WRITING FRACTIONS

Write the fraction of the shape that is filled in.

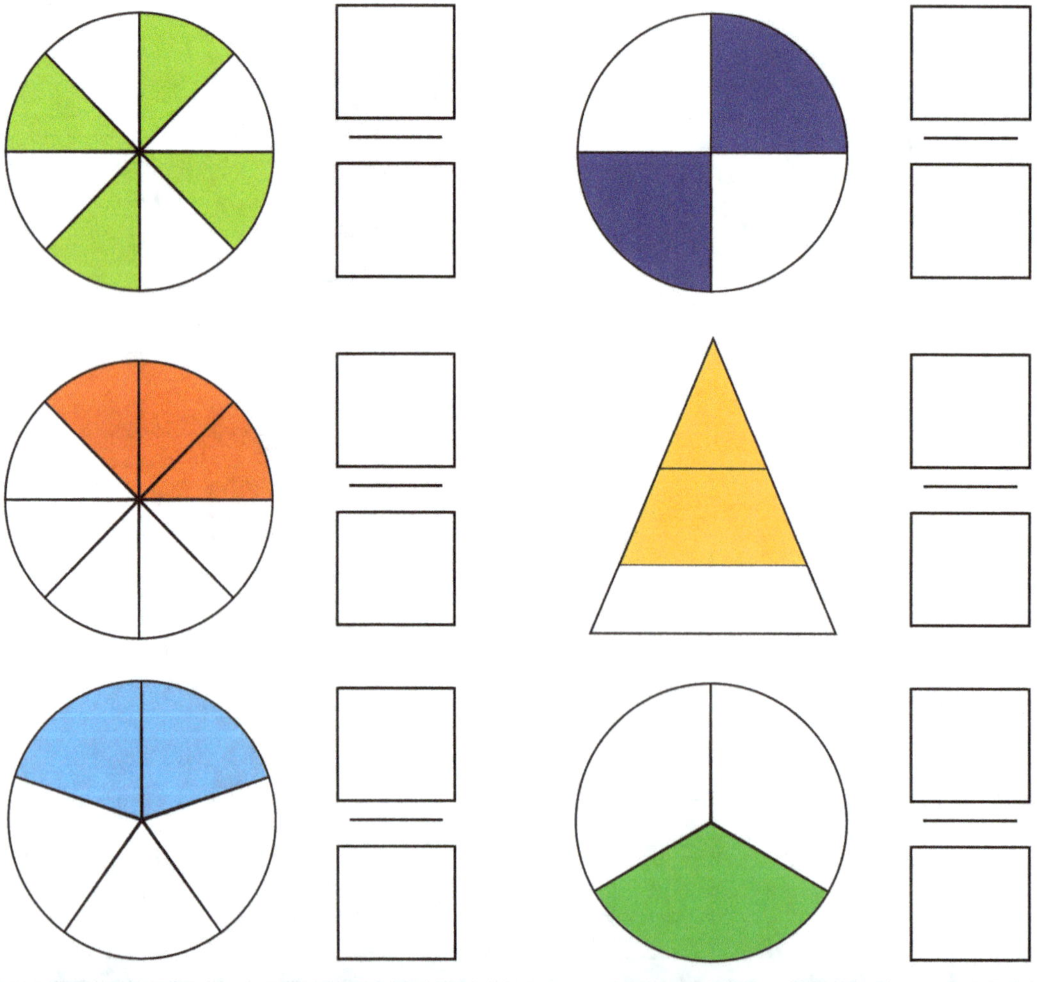

WRITING FRACTIONS

Write the fraction of the shape that is filled in.

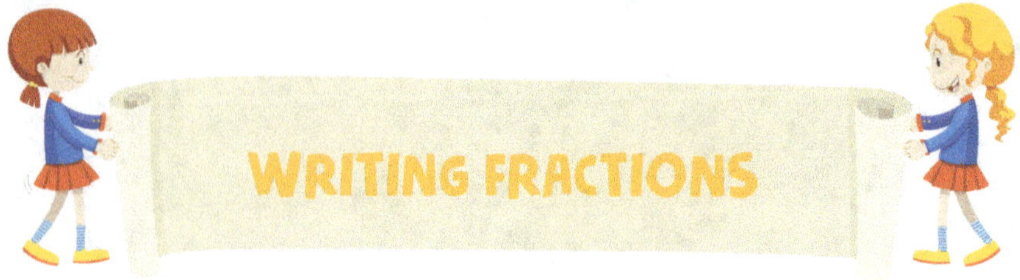

WRITING FRACTIONS

Write the fraction of the shape that is filled in.

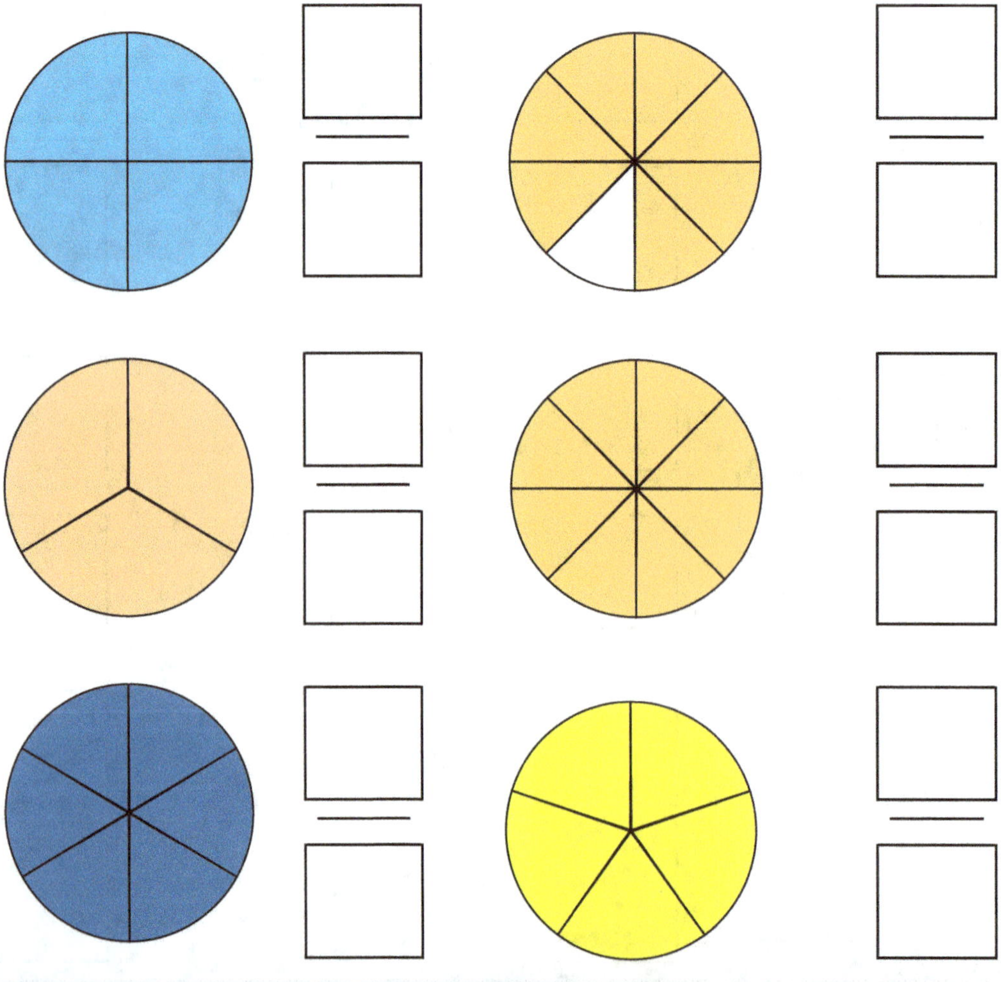

WRITING FRACTIONS

Write the fraction of the shape that is filled in.

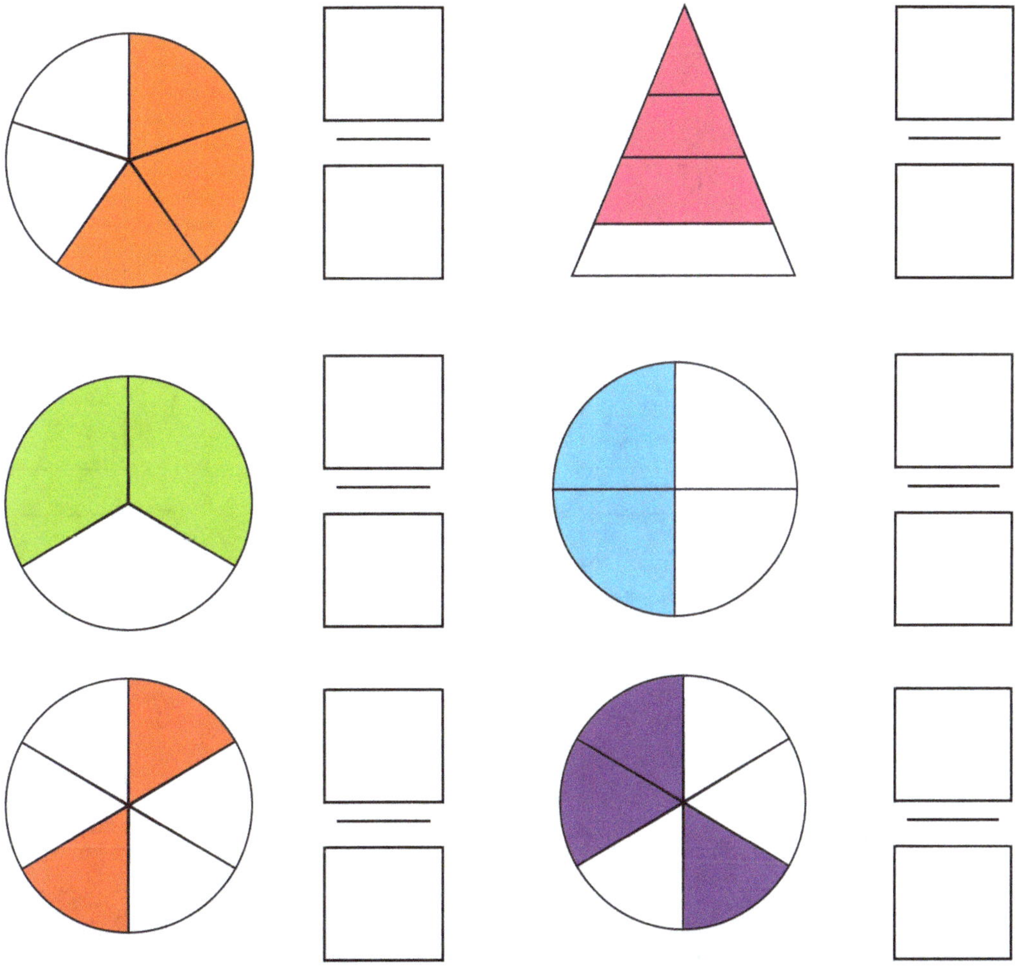

WRITING FRACTIONS

Write the fraction of the shape that is filled in.

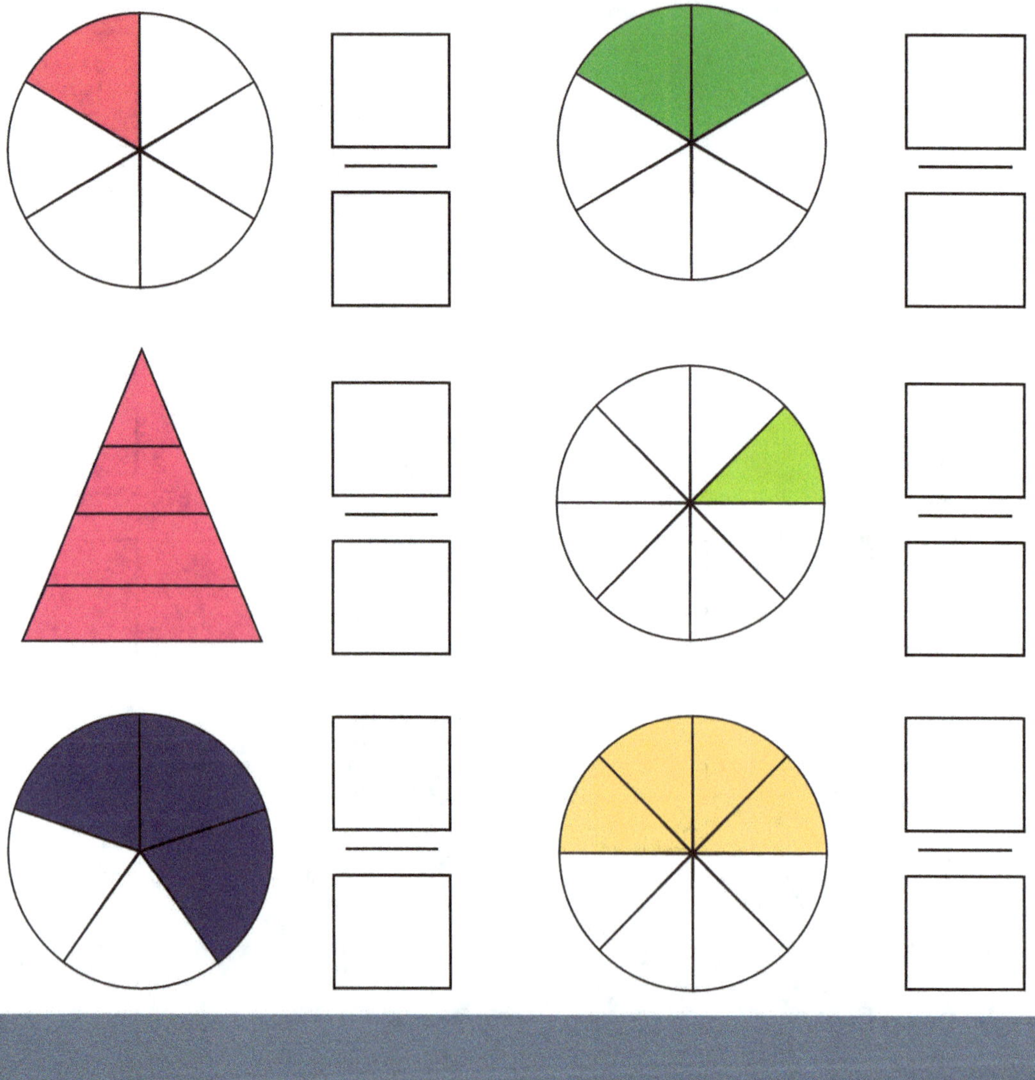

NAMING FRACTIONS

Determine which letter best describes the shaded portion.

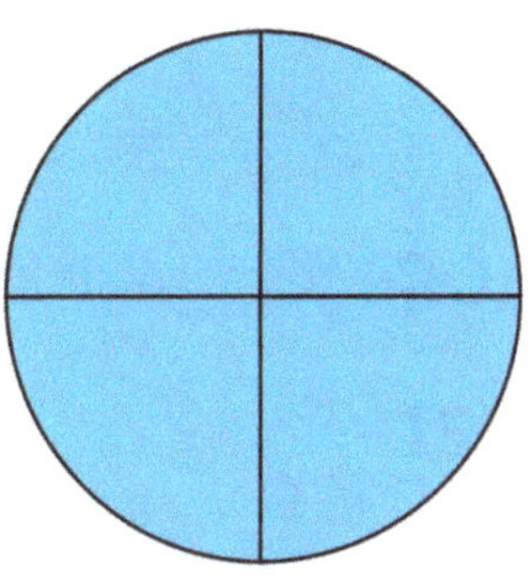

A. Two Quarters

B. Four Quarters

C. One Quarter

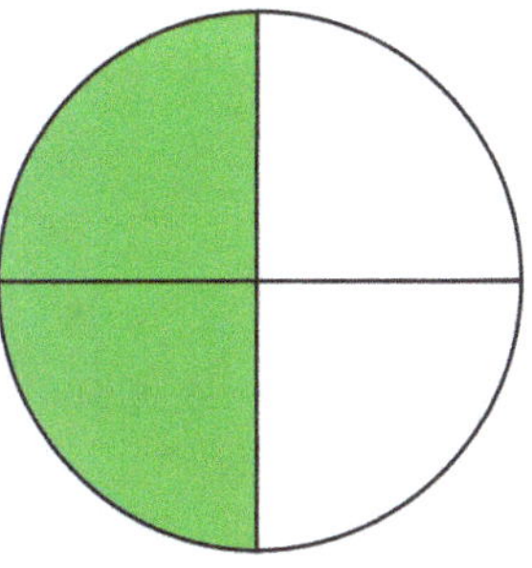

A. Two Quarters

B. One Quarter

C. Three Quarters

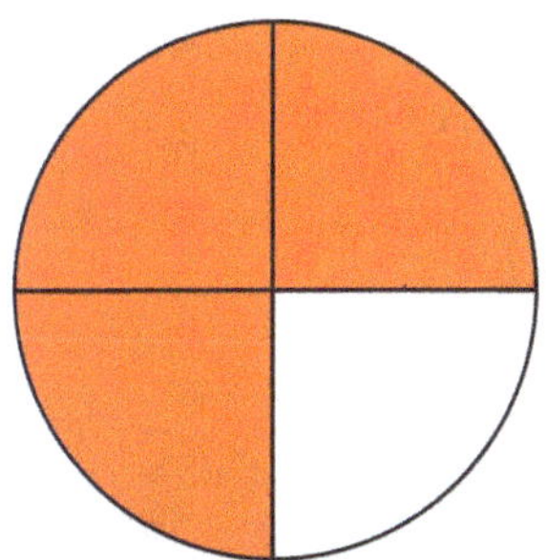

A. Two Quarters

B. One Quarter

C. Three Quarters

NAMING FRACTIONS

Determine which letter best describes the shaded portion.

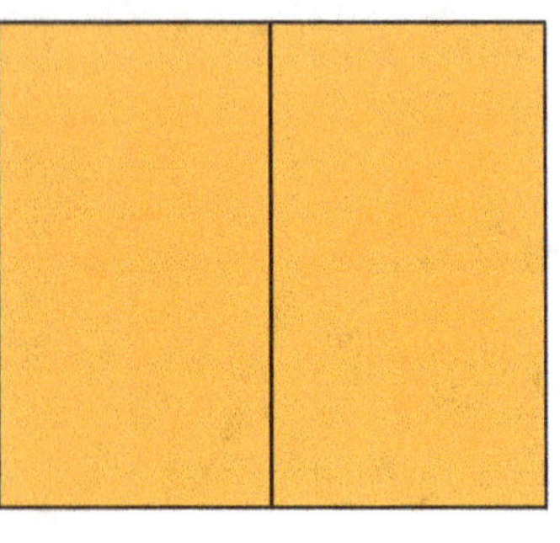

A. Two Halves

B. Two Quarters

C. One Quarter

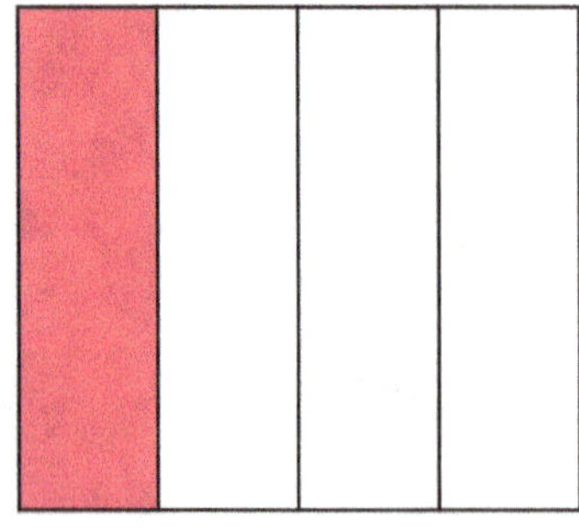

A. Two Quarters

B. One Quarter

C. Three Quarters

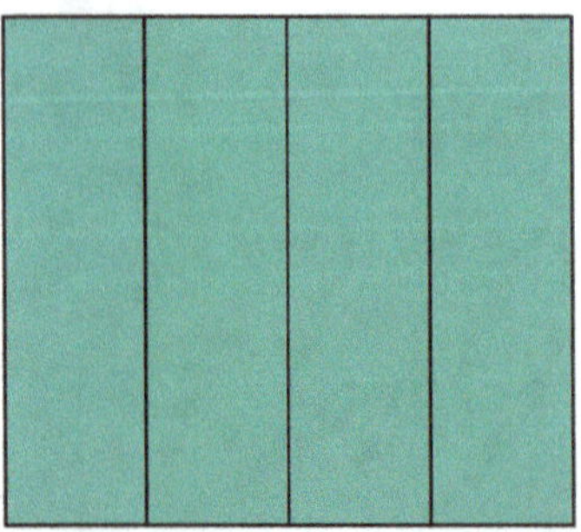

A. Two Quarters

B. Four-Fourths

C. One Quarter

NAMING FRACTIONS

Determine which letter best describes the shaded portion.

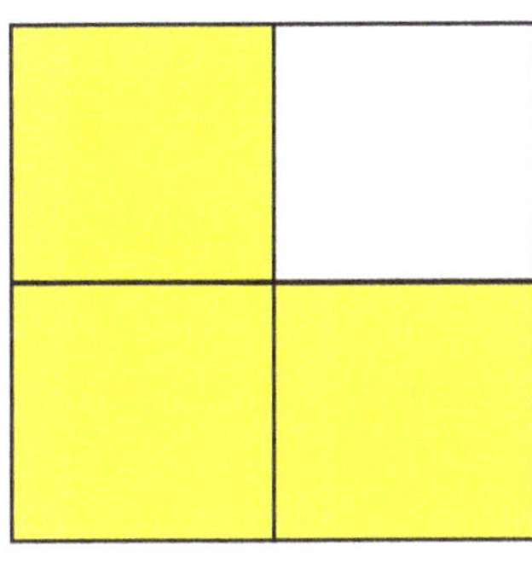

A. One Quarter
B. Three-Fourths
C. Two Quarters

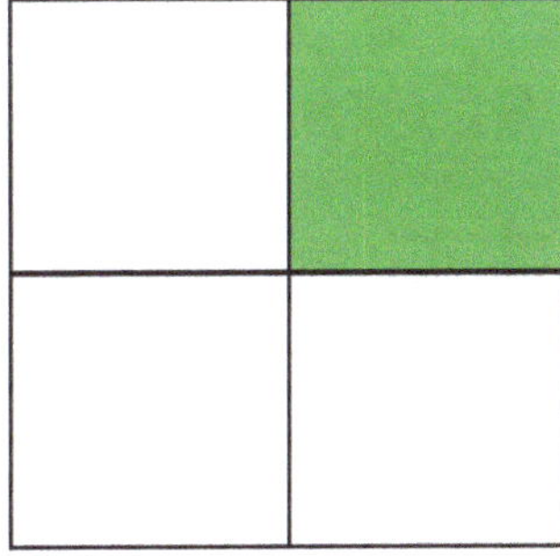

A. Three Quarters
B. Two Quarters
C. One Quarter

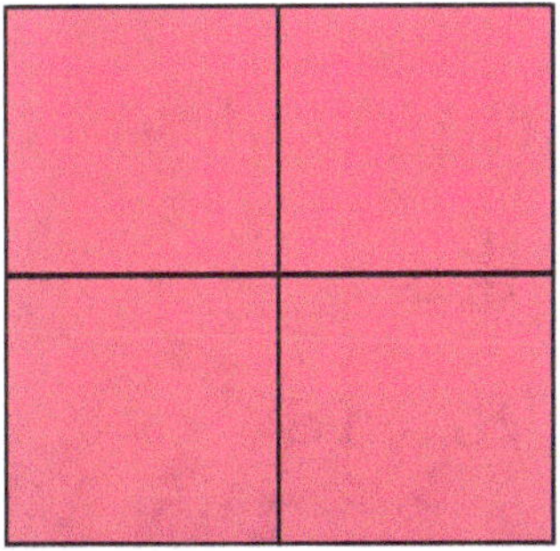

A. Four Quarters
B. One Quarter
C. Two Quarters

NAMING FRACTIONS

Determine which letter best describes the shaded portion.

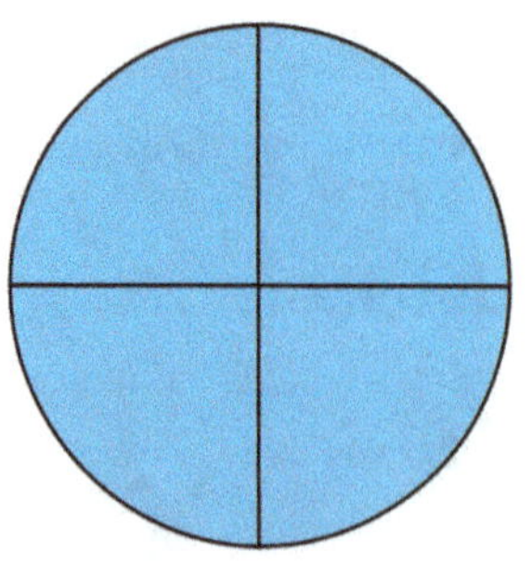

A. One Quarter

B. Four Quarters

C. Two Quarters

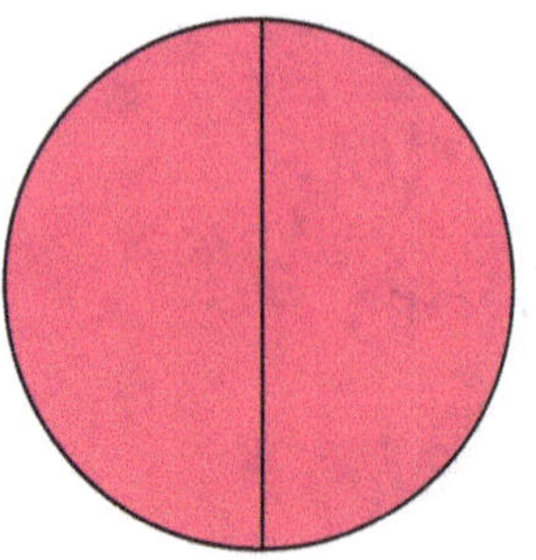

A. Three Quarters

B. One Quarter

C. Two Quarters

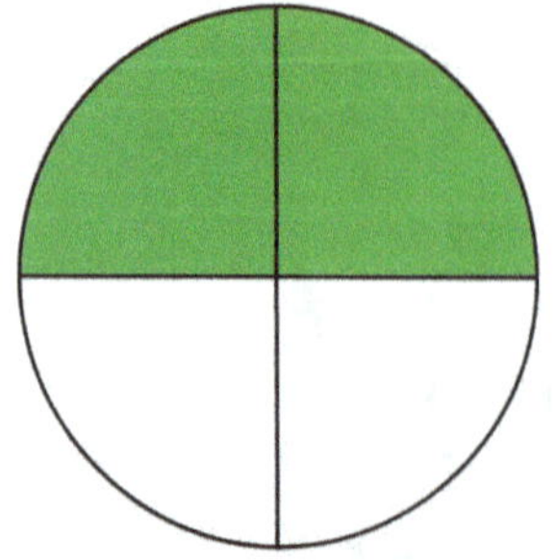

A. One Quarter

B. Two-Fourths

C. Three Quarters

NAMING FRACTIONS

Determine which letter best describes the shaded portion.

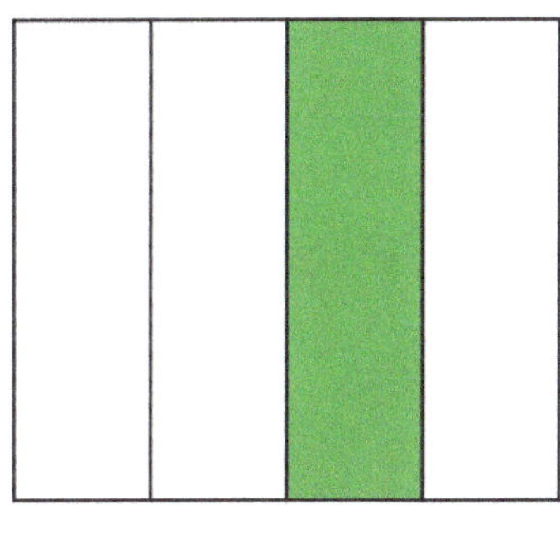

A. Three Quarters

B. Two Quarters

C. One-Fourth

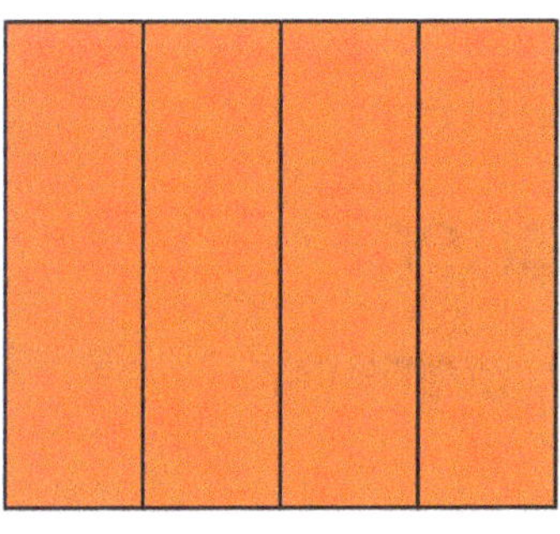

A. Two Quarters

B. One Quarter

C. Four Quarters

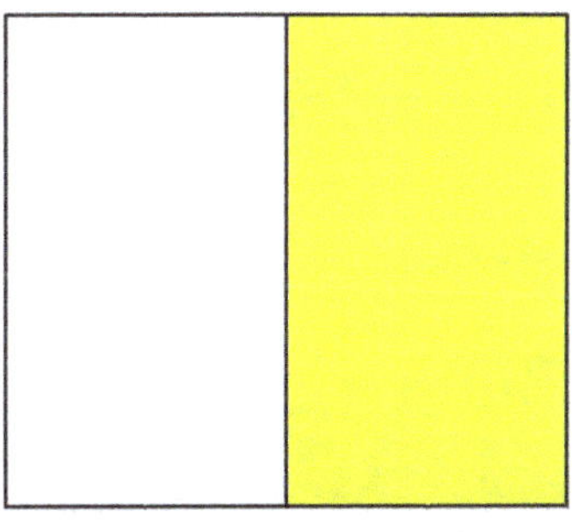

A. Three Quarters

B. One Quarter

C. One Half

NAMING FRACTIONS

Determine which letter best describes the shaded portion.

A. One Quarter

B. Three Quarters

C. Two Quarters

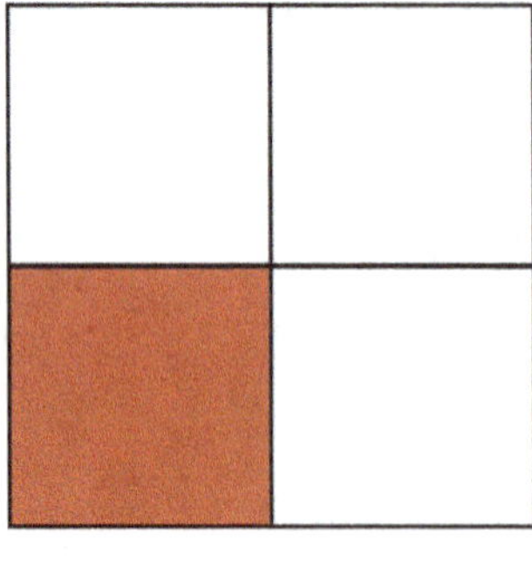

A. One Quarter

B. Two Quarters

C. Three Quarters

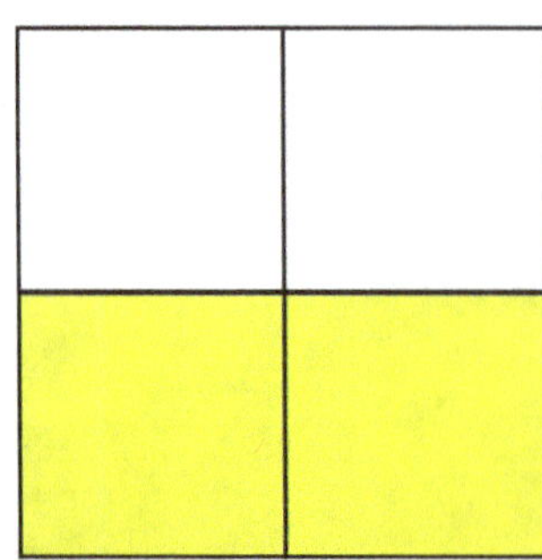

A. Three Quarters

B. Two-Fourths

C. One Quarter

NAMING FRACTIONS

Determine which letter best describes the shaded portion.

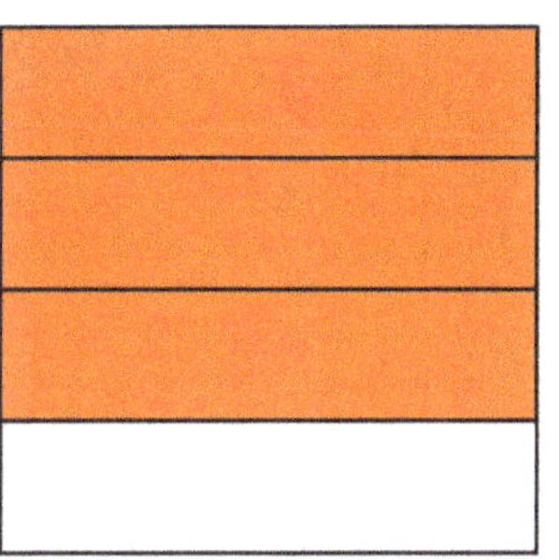

A. One Quarter
B. Two Quarters
C. Three Quarters

A. Two Quarters
B. Four Quarters
C. One Quarter

A. One Quarter
B. Two Quarters
C. Three Quarters

answer keys

What fraction of each shape is colored?
Circle the correct answer.

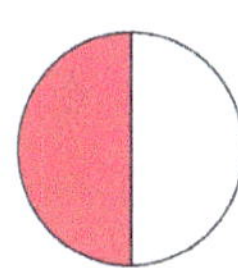

 $\frac{1}{4}$  $\frac{1}{2}$ $\frac{2}{4}$ 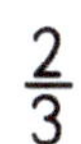 $\frac{2}{3}$

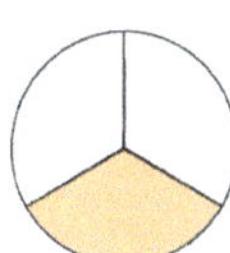

$\frac{1}{4}$ 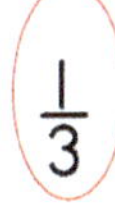 $\frac{1}{3}$ $\frac{3}{3}$ 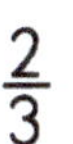 $\frac{2}{3}$

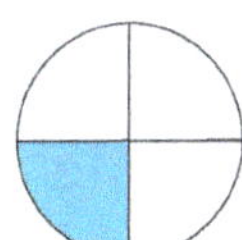

$\frac{1}{4}$ $\frac{2}{3}$ $\frac{2}{4}$ $\frac{4}{4}$

What fraction of each shape is colored?
Circle the correct answer.

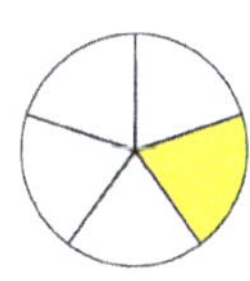

$\frac{1}{5}$ $\frac{1}{7}$ $\frac{4}{6}$ $\frac{2}{4}$

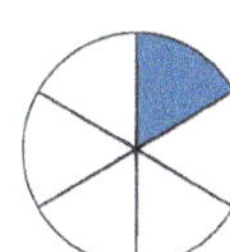

$\frac{1}{4}$ $\frac{1}{3}$ $\frac{3}{5}$ $\frac{1}{6}$

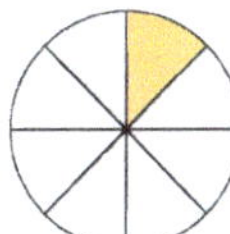

$\frac{1}{4}$ $\frac{2}{3}$ $\frac{1}{8}$ $\frac{4}{4}$

What fraction of each shape is colored?
Circle the correct answer.

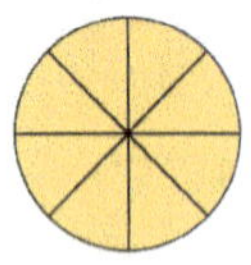

$\frac{1}{4}$ $\frac{5}{5}$ $\frac{8}{8}$ $\frac{3}{4}$

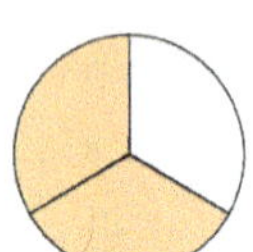

$\frac{4}{4}$ $\frac{1}{3}$ $\frac{3}{3}$ $\frac{2}{3}$

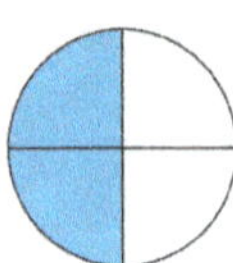

$\frac{1}{4}$ $\frac{2}{3}$ $\frac{2}{4}$ $\frac{6}{6}$

MATCHING FRACTIONS
TO A PICTURE

What fraction of each shape is colored?
Circle the correct answer.

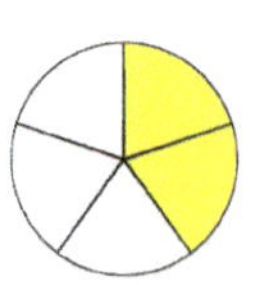

$\frac{5}{7}$ $\frac{1}{2}$ $\frac{2}{5}$ $\frac{2}{3}$

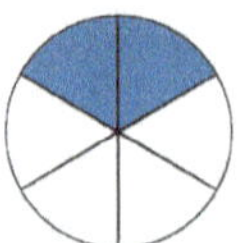

$\frac{1}{4}$ $\frac{2}{6}$ $\frac{3}{3}$ $\frac{5}{7}$

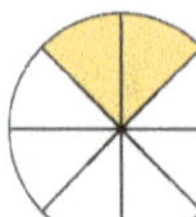

$\frac{2}{8}$ $\frac{2}{3}$ $\frac{2}{4}$ $\frac{4}{7}$

What fraction of each shape is colored?
Circle the correct answer.

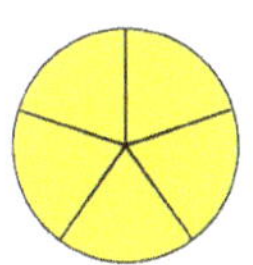

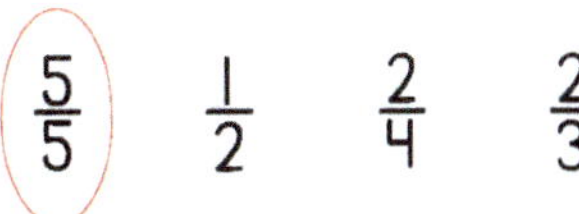

$\frac{5}{5}$ $\frac{1}{2}$ $\frac{2}{4}$ $\frac{2}{3}$

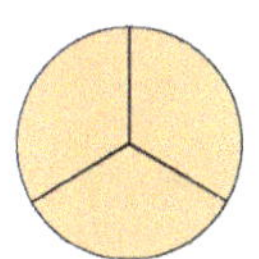

$\frac{1}{4}$ $\frac{1}{3}$ $\frac{3}{3}$ $\frac{4}{5}$

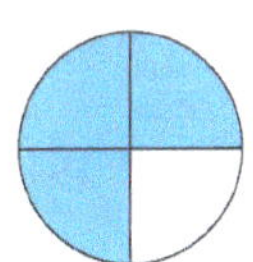

$\frac{1}{4}$ $\frac{2}{3}$ $\frac{2}{4}$ $\frac{3}{4}$

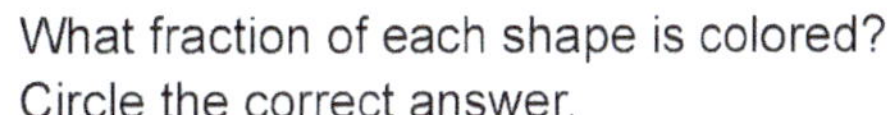

What fraction of each shape is colored?
Circle the correct answer.

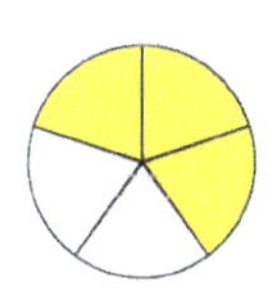

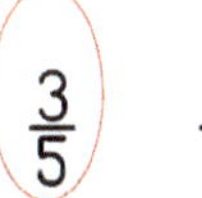

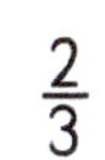

$\frac{4}{7}$ $\frac{1}{2}$ $\frac{3}{5}$ $\frac{2}{3}$

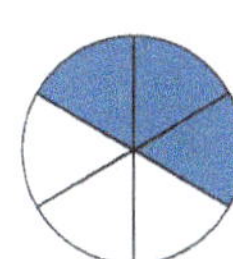

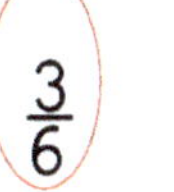

$\frac{1}{4}$ $\frac{1}{3}$ $\frac{3}{6}$ $\frac{3}{7}$

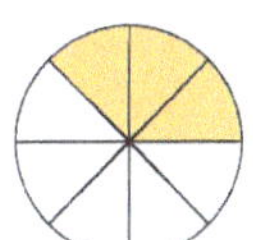

$\frac{1}{4}$ $\frac{3}{8}$ $\frac{2}{4}$ $\frac{6}{8}$

What fraction of each shape is colored?
Circle the correct answer.

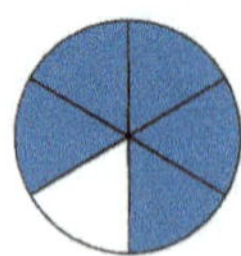

$\frac{6}{7}$ $\frac{1}{2}$ $\frac{5}{6}$ $\frac{2}{3}$

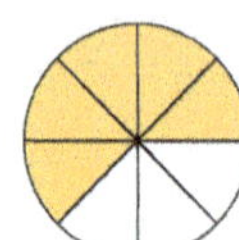

$\frac{5}{8}$ $\frac{1}{3}$ $\frac{3}{3}$ $\frac{5}{7}$

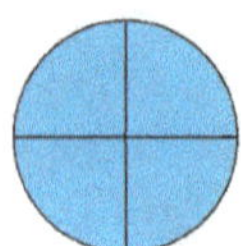

$\frac{1}{4}$ $\frac{2}{3}$ $\frac{2}{4}$ 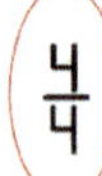 $\frac{4}{4}$

What fraction of each shape is colored?
Circle the correct answer.

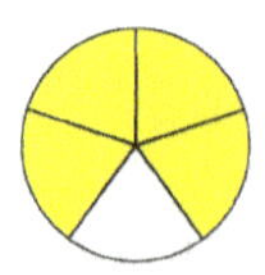

$\frac{4}{5}$ $\frac{1}{2}$ $\frac{1}{6}$ $\frac{5}{6}$

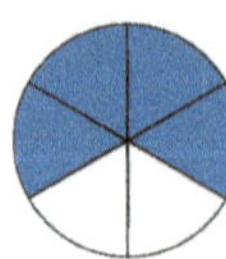

$\frac{1}{4}$ $\frac{4}{6}$ $\frac{3}{3}$ $\frac{6}{6}$

$\frac{4}{8}$ $\frac{2}{3}$ $\frac{2}{4}$ $\frac{6}{7}$

What fraction of each shape is colored?
Circle the correct answer.

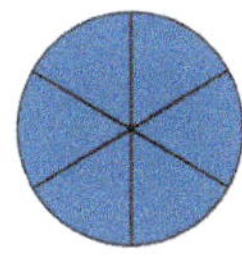

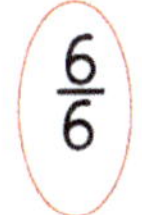 $\frac{6}{6}$ $\frac{1}{2}$ $\frac{2}{4}$ $\frac{1}{6}$

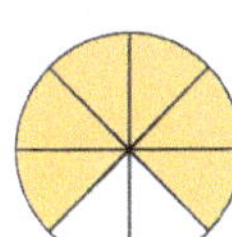

$\frac{8}{9}$ $\frac{1}{3}$ $\frac{3}{3}$ $\frac{6}{8}$

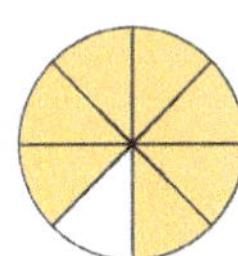

$\frac{1}{4}$ $\frac{5}{6}$ $\frac{2}{4}$ $\frac{7}{8}$

What fraction of each shape is colored?
Circle the correct answer.

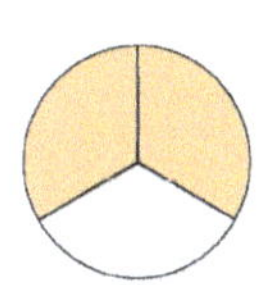

$\frac{5}{5}$ $\frac{1}{2}$ $\frac{2}{4}$ $\frac{2}{3}$

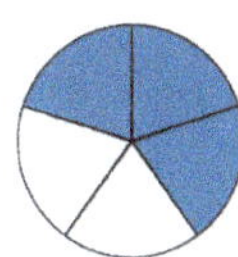

$\frac{3}{5}$ $\frac{1}{3}$ $\frac{3}{3}$ $\frac{5}{6}$

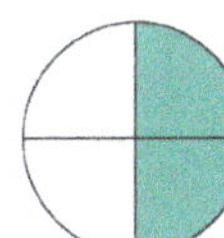

$\frac{4}{7}$ $\frac{2}{3}$ $\frac{2}{4}$ $\frac{3}{4}$

Color in the fraction shown of each picture.

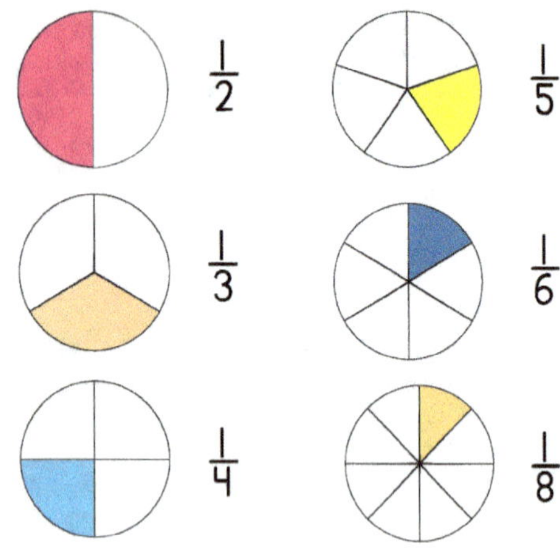

Color in the fraction shown of each picture.

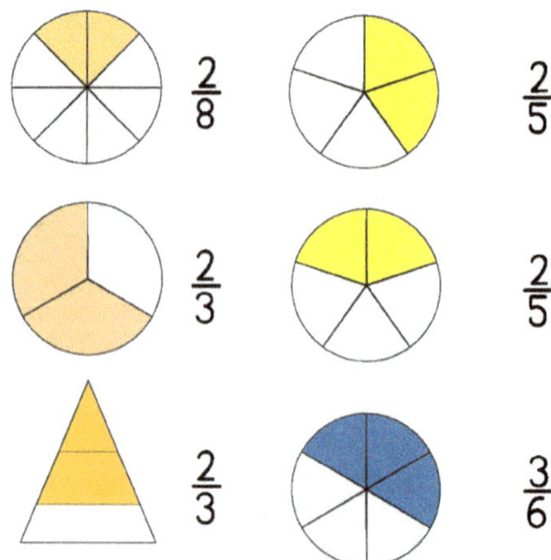

Color in the fraction shown of each picture.

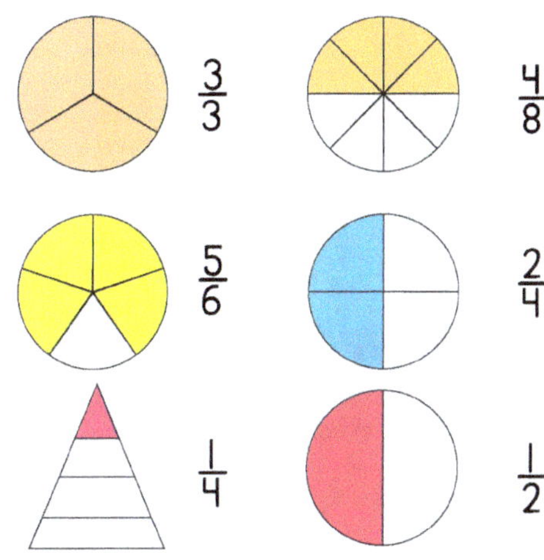

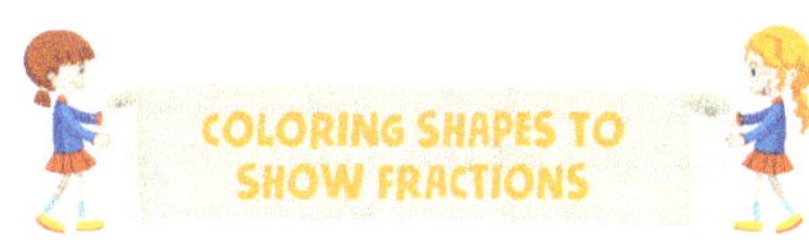

Color in the fraction shown of each picture.

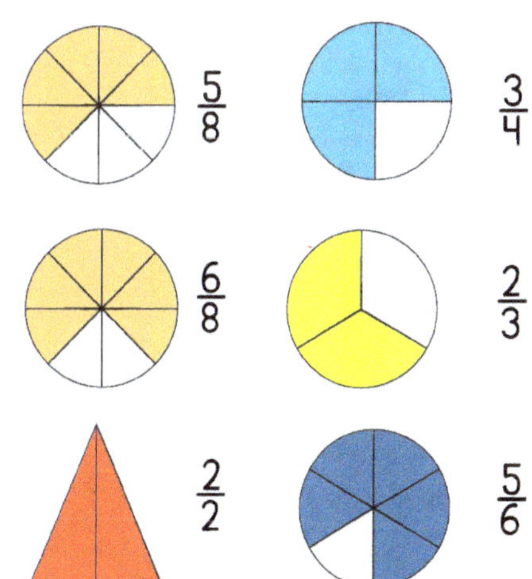

Color in the fraction shown of each picture.

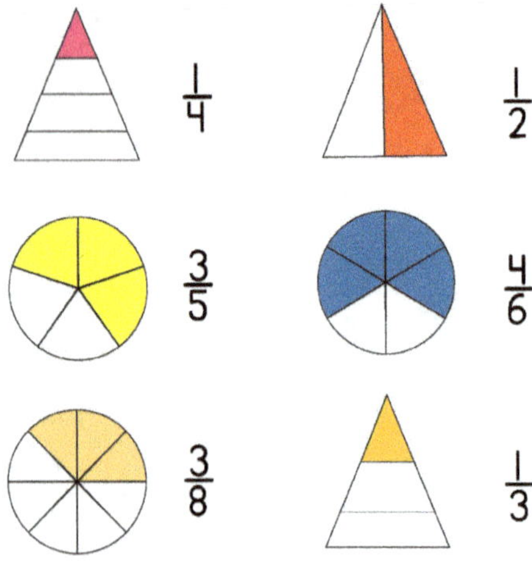

Color in the fraction shown of each picture.

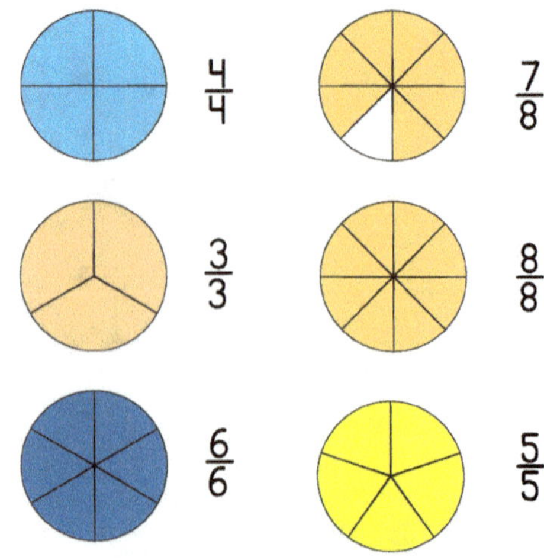

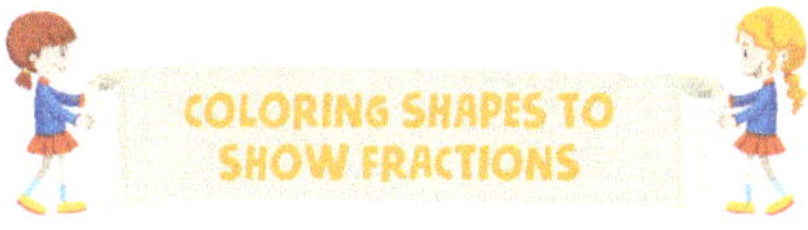

Color in the fraction shown of each picture.

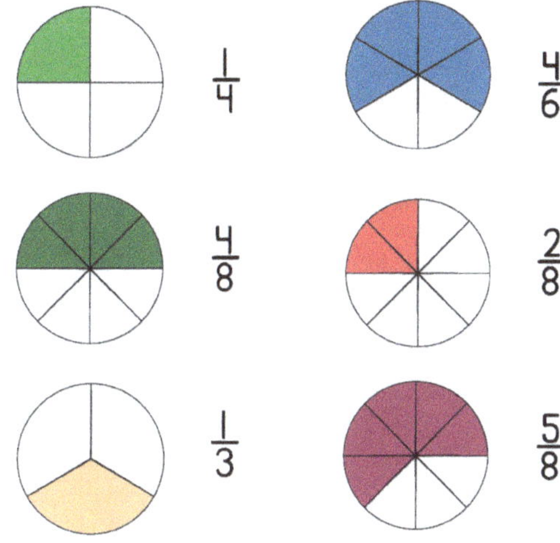

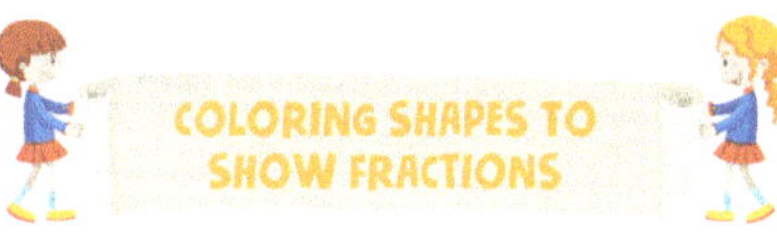

Color in the fraction shown of each picture.

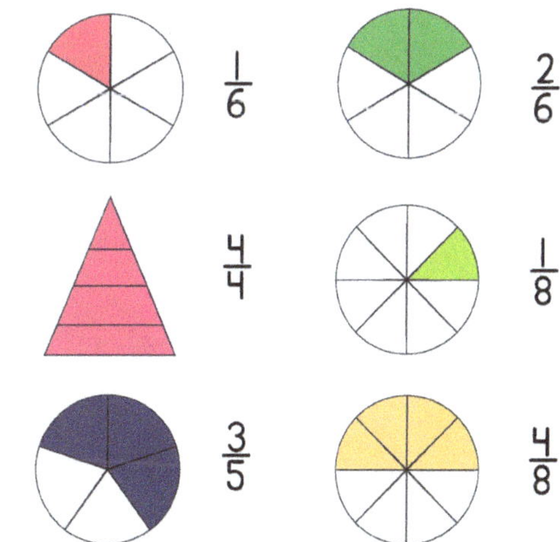

Color in the fraction shown of each picture.

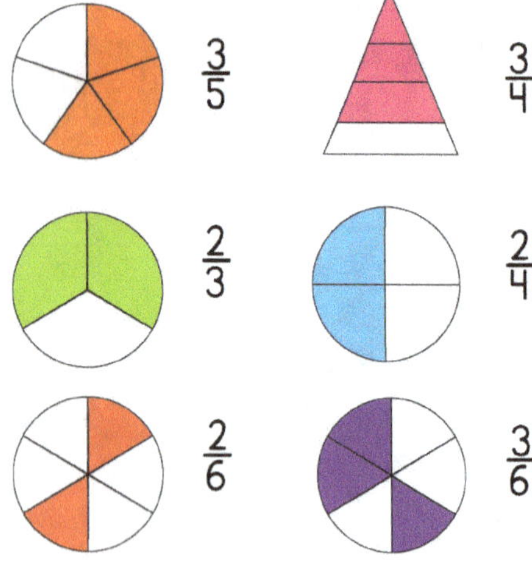

Color in the fraction shown of each picture.

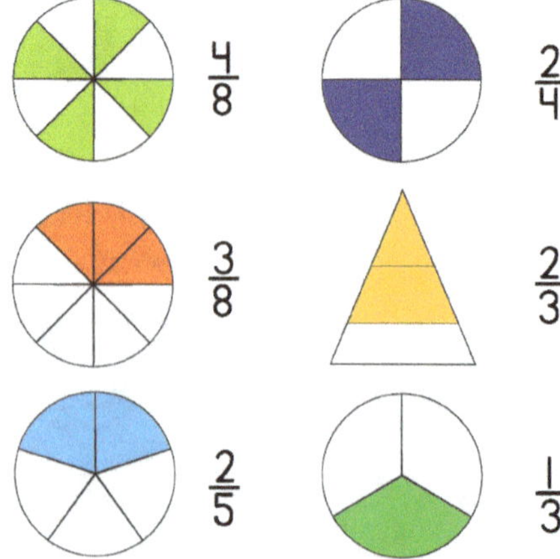

Write the fraction of the shape that is filled in.

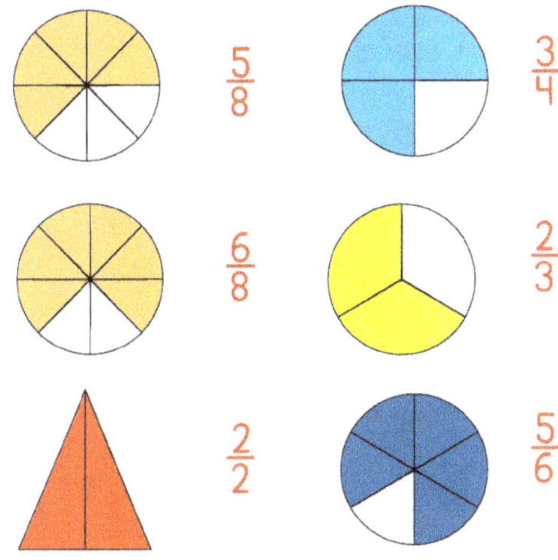

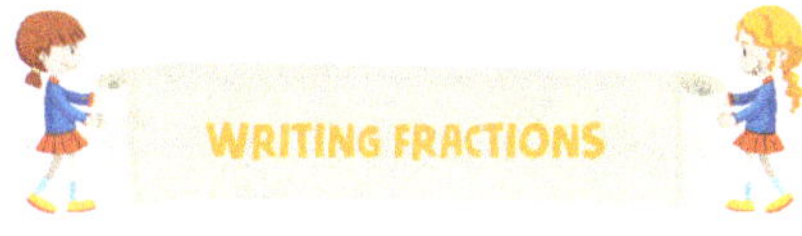

Write the fraction of the shape that is filled in.

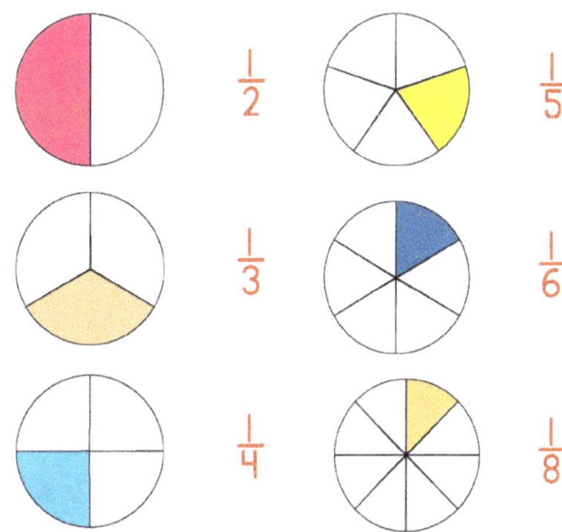

Write the fraction of the shape that is filled in.

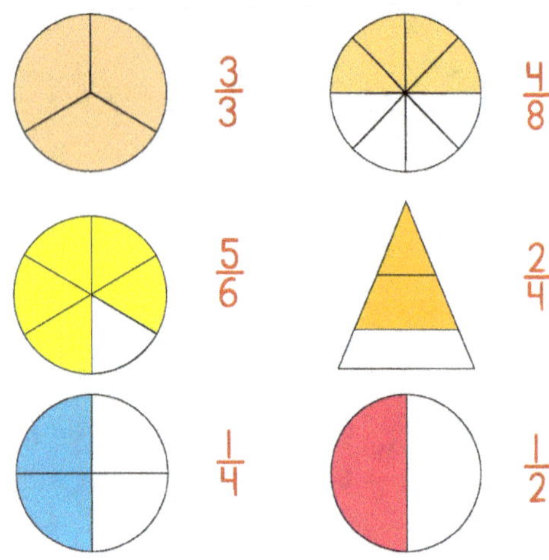

Write the fraction of the shape that is filled in.

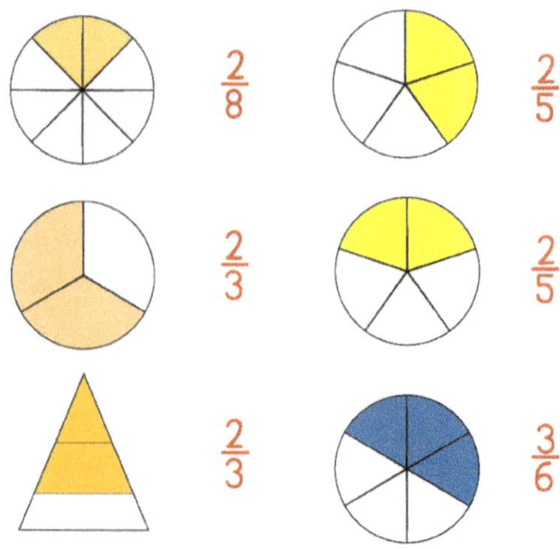

Write the fraction of the shape that is filled in.

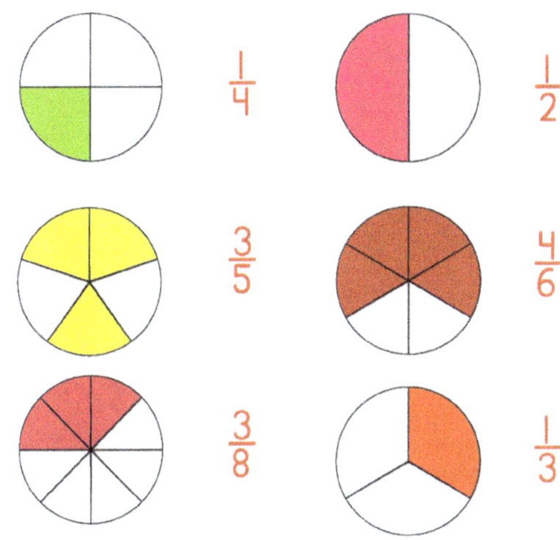

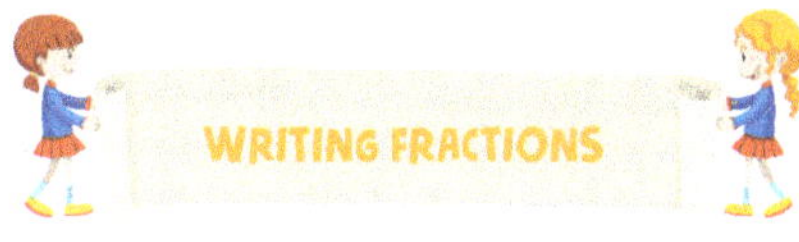

Write the fraction of the shape that is filled in.

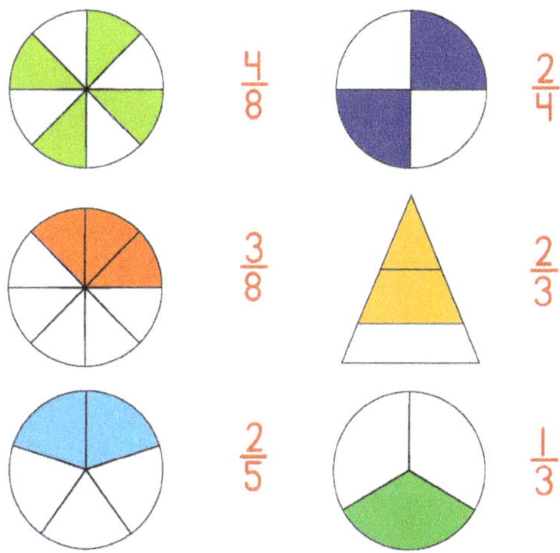

Write the fraction of the shape that is filled in.

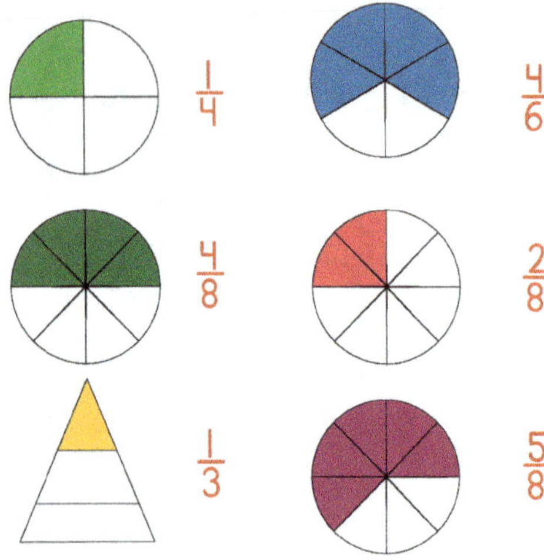

Write the fraction of the shape that is filled in.

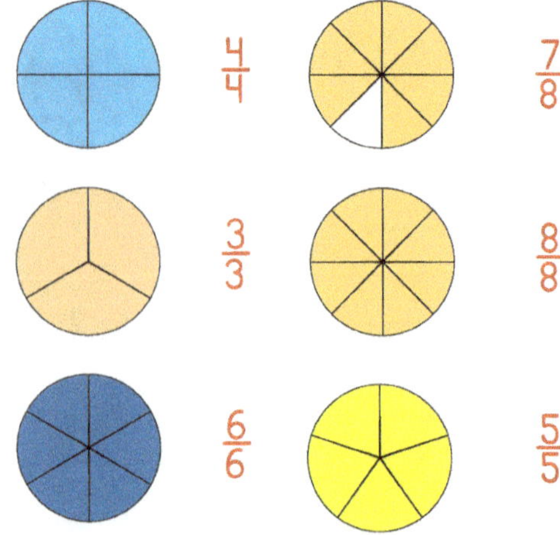

Write the fraction of the shape that is filled in.

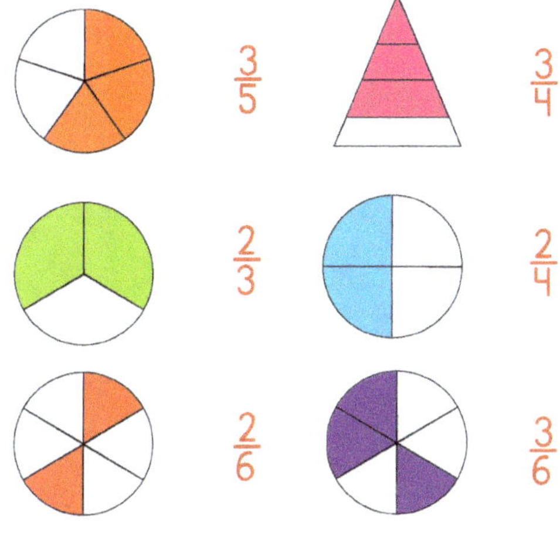

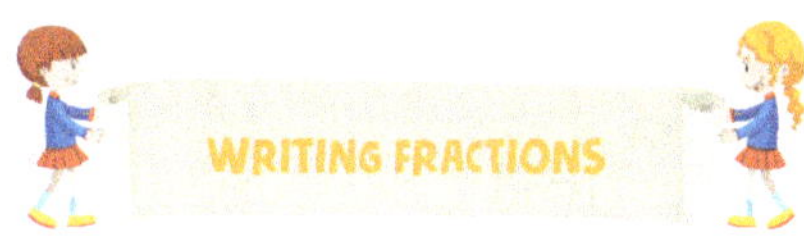

Write the fraction of the shape that is filled in.

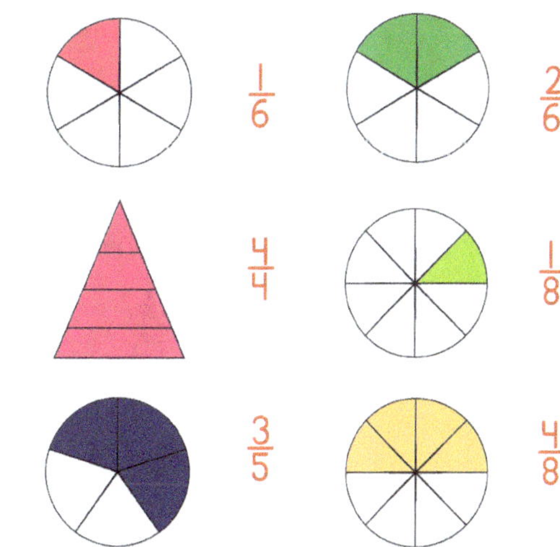

Determine which letter best describes the shaded portion.

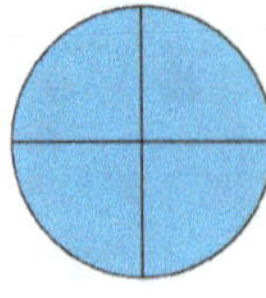

A. Two Quarters
B. Four Quarters
C. One Quarter

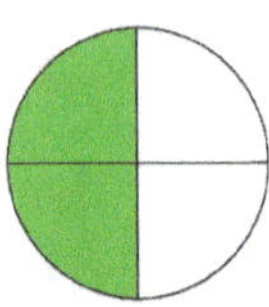

A. Two Quarters
B. One Quarter
C. Three Quarters

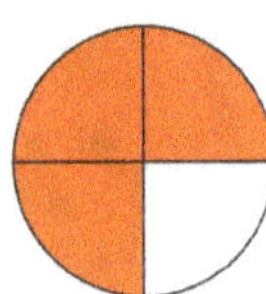

A. Two Quarters
B. One Quarter
C. Three Quarters

Determine which letter best describes the shaded portion.

A. Two Halves
B. Two Quarters
C. One Quarter

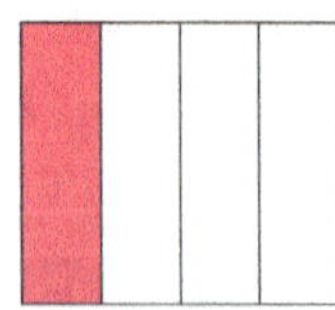

A. Two Quarters
B. One Quarter
C. Three Quarters

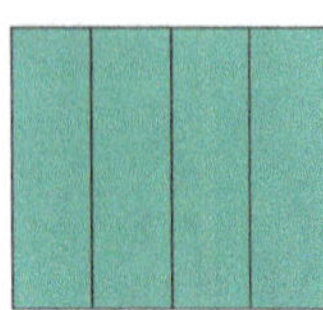

A. Two Quarters
B. Four-Fourths
C. One Quarter

Determine which letter best describes the shaded portion.

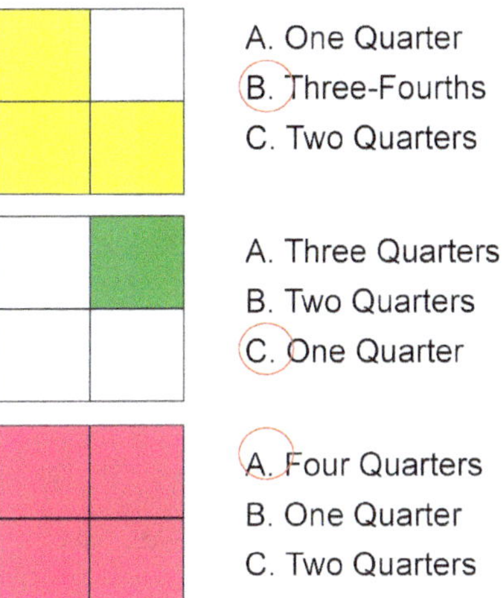

A. One Quarter
B. Three-Fourths
C. Two Quarters

A. Three Quarters
B. Two Quarters
C. One Quarter

A. Four Quarters
B. One Quarter
C. Two Quarters

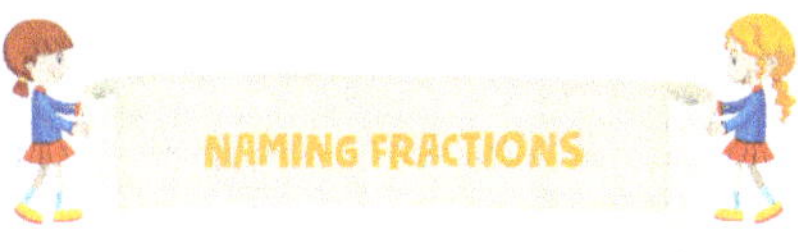

Determine which letter best describes the shaded portion.

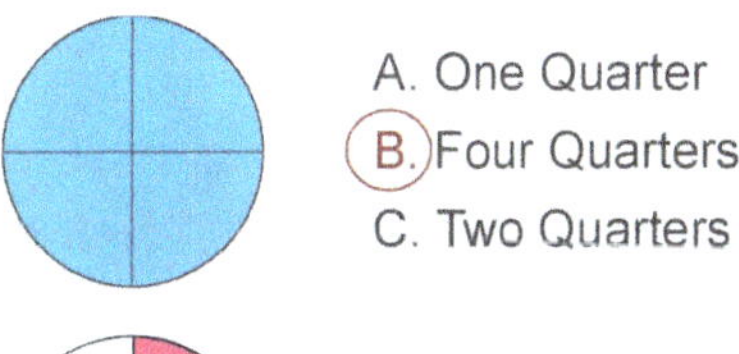

A. One Quarter
B. Four Quarters
C. Two Quarters

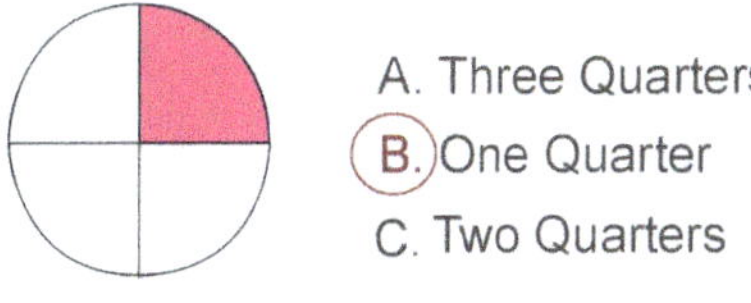

A. Three Quarters
B. One Quarter
C. Two Quarters

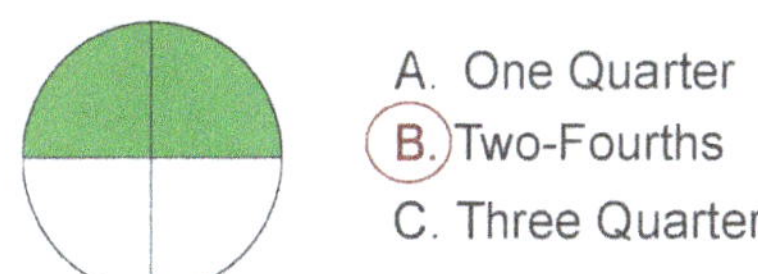

A. One Quarter
B. Two-Fourths
C. Three Quarters

Determine which letter best describes the shaded portion.

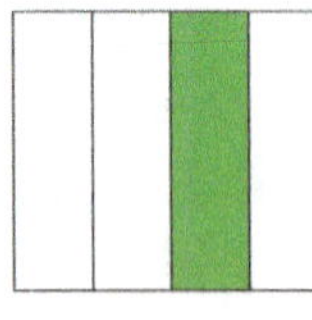

A. Three Quarters
B. Two Quarters
C. One-Fourth

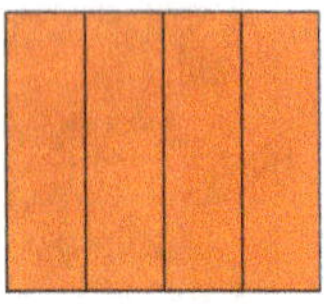

A. Two Quarters
B. One Quarter
C. Four Quarters

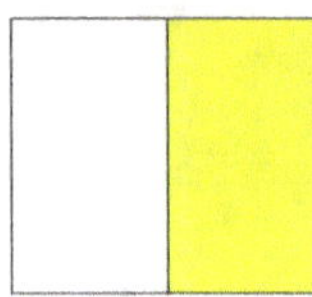

A. Three Quarters
B. One Quarter
C. One Half

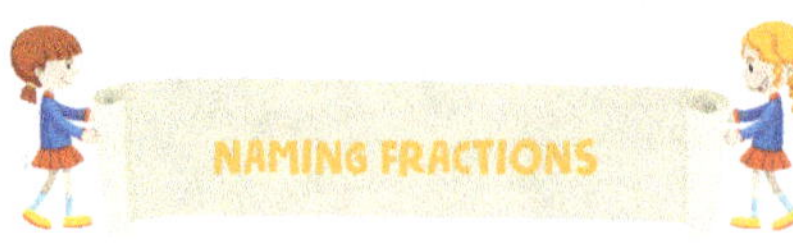

Determine which letter best describes the shaded portion.

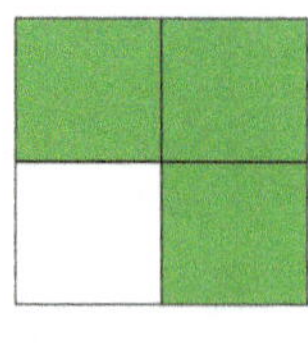

A. One Quarter
B. Three Quarters
C. Two Quarters

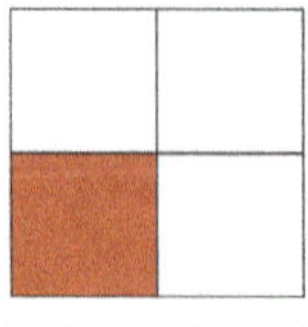

A. One Quarter
B. Two Quarters
C. Three Quarters

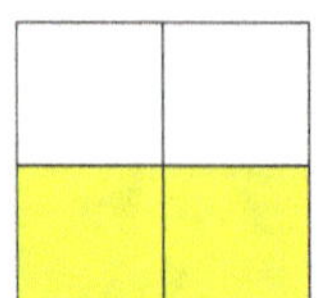

A. Three Quarters
B. Two-Fourths
C. One Quarter

Determine which letter best describes the shaded portion.

A. One Quarter
B. Two Quarters
C. Three Quarters

A. Two Quarters
B. Four Quarters
C. One Quarter

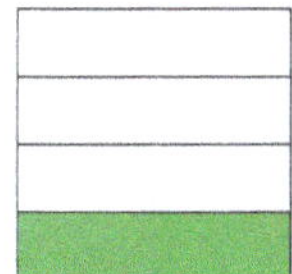

A. One Quarter
B. Two Quarters
C. Three Quarters

www.ingramcontent.com/pod-product-compliance
Lightning Source LLC
LaVergne TN
LVHW060506170826
845677LV00026B/1629
* 9 7 9 8 8 6 9 4 4 1 4 3 0 *